HOW TO
WRITE

ARTICLES FOR NEWSPAPERS AND MAGAZINES

HOW TO
WRITE

ARTICLES FOR NEWSPAPERS AND MAGAZINES

Dawn B. Sova, Ph.D.

MACMILLAN • USA

Also in ARCO's How to Series:

How to Interpret Poetry
How to Read and Write About Drama
How to Read and Write About Fiction
How to Write and Deliver an Effective Speech
How to Write Book Reports
How to Write Poetry
How to Write Research Papers
How to Write Short Stories
How to Write Themes and Essays
How to Write a Thesis

Macmillan Reference USA
A Simon & Schuster Macmillan Company
1633 Broadway
New York, NY 10019

Macmillan Publishing books may be purchased for business or sales promotional use. For information please write: Special Markets Department, Macmillan Publishing USA, 1633 Broadway, New York, NY 10019.

An Arco Book

ARCO is a registered trademark of Simon & Schuster, Inc.
MACMILLAN is a registered trademark of Macmillan, Inc.

Library of Congress Catalog Card Number: 97-80142

ISBN: 0-02-862190-5

Manufactured in the United States of America

10   9   8   7   6   5   4   3   2   1

Contents

Chapter One

Getting Started

Writing articles for newspapers and magazines requires that you take careful steps in developing ideas, planning the article, collecting information and focusing on the subject. You should do all of these steps before you write the first draft of the *lead*—the opening paragraph(s) of a news article that succinctly summarize(s) the material that follows. Nonfiction markets for newspapers and magazines focus on the real world, but it is a selective reality. Thus, the power of an article derives from the extent to which the writer selects from a myriad of facts, and the manner in which those facts are arranged.

A major difference between the newspaper article market and the magazine article market lies in the source of the topic. Newspaper articles are usually assigned, based on breaking news, local interests and the nature of the market. In contrast, magazine articles often begin life as freelance queries, a writer's idea that is pitched to the editor of a specific magazine. In some cases, editors will assign articles to writers with whom they have worked before and who have developed reputations for good writing, attention to deadlines and accuracy of facts.

Newspapers publish both *hard news* and *soft news* articles; each type calls for a different commitment, approach and result from the writer. The hard news article requires that a writer move fast to capture the immediacy of the event. Such accounts must tell the reader what has happened, is happening or will happen, as well as give a careful report of the why and how behind the occurrence. The journalistic "5 Ws + H"—who, what, when, where, why and how—applies here. The hard news article presents a factual account of an event, without significant attention to the reactions of observers or participants, although quotes along these lines might appear. The people involved and how they are affected *now* are also important.

Soft news or *feature* articles do not have the same time or subject restrictions. Profiles of noteworthy people, human interest stories and discussions of issues are examples of feature stories. Consumer, self-help, entertaining and inspirational stories are other examples. Aside from the hard news sections of weekly newsmagazines such as *Time*, *Newsweek* and *U.S. News and World Report*, most magazine articles are features because their publication schedules require from several days to several weeks of lead time (the time elapsed between acceptance of work and publication), which is also true for their hard news articles.

GENERATING IDEAS

Story ideas rarely wait for a writer to appear, although writers are occasionally fortunate to be present and ready to take notes when a news story breaks. If you are on the scene at a breaking story, sharpen your senses to make certain that you report accurately all that you and everyone else involved see, hear, smell and feel. Observe closely and decide just where the story lies; then be prepared to take careful steps to sort through the numerous ideas that are certain to accumulate.

Ideas for most newspaper and magazine articles arise in a more mundane manner. Some topics might have only local interest, but many more issues and ideas also arise in other communities and have national implications. The trick is in taking a wide-angle view of the situation and in narrowing your focus to only the one aspect of the situation. Several ways of gaining writing ideas are helpful:

1. Observe the people and places around you.
2. Talk with people and listen to their conversations.
3. Examine local and national concerns.
4. Consider an issue from different points of view.

5. Divide broader topics into their components.
6. Pay attention to new and established local programs.
7. Read the personal and classified advertisements.
8. Review your "interesting article ideas" files.

1. Observe the people and places around you.
Look around and find something that interests or intrigues you. The same topic might also interest or intrigue both local and national readers.

- Have you always wondered about the history of an oddly shaped or strangely decorated building? Was the octagon shape a popular architectural style in your area or nationwide?
- Do you know why the local high school's sports teams are named the Boilermakers? Are there other unusual high school team names in your area or nationwide?
- Does a street in your community have an unusual name—or one that is pronounced in an unorthodox manner? What is "Pierre Avenue" doing in a town settled mostly by Polish and Italian immigrants, and why is it pronounced "Peery Avenue"? Do area towns have similarly unusual street names?
- What is the source of an old local landmark? Who maintains it? For whom does it still have meaning? Does it represent a bygone era? Is the landmark unique, or is it a period piece that might be found in other towns in the area or nationwide?

2. Talk with people and listen to their conversations.
Ask your family members and friends what issues and ideas concern or interest them; then learn more about those issues and ideas.

- Are people curious or worried about the direction that the newly proposed building project will take, now that the mayor and the city council have been voted out of office? How do other towns handle the problem? What is happening nationwide?
- Does a friend sometimes muse about the origin of the amphitheater on campus and question why a college would invest in such an im-

posing outdoor structure? What other massive structures appear on your campus or on nearby campuses? How many other colleges nationwide have an amphitheater modeled on those of ancient Greece?

- Do family members often talk about the large number of variations of your surname and question how closely individuals with name variations are actually related?

3. Examine local and national concerns.

Read national and local papers to identify issues that can be adapted to both levels of concern. Many issues only require the involvement of nearby residents to turn a broad national concern into one of local interest. In contrast, a local concern can take on national interest when it is found to affect the lives of individuals with diverse backgrounds and geographical locations.

- Will the national concern with a future crisis in the funding of Social Security have a serious affect on current retirees, as well as those about to retire, in your community or family? What worries are expressed by younger workers having 20 or more years left in the workforce?
- Does the change in the types of cases that come before the municipal court in your town indicate only a local trend? Or are similar-size cities nationwide reporting an increase in certain cases?
- What impact will a move of the Federal Reserve Board to increase interest rates have on college students and their families? Will college loans and tuition costs be affected negatively or positively?

4. Consider an issue from different points of view.

Place yourself in someone else's role when looking at a specific issue. Identify what your new view of the issue might be and how it would affect your life.

- Has a local building project promised to aid the town economy by adding jobs and store sales? What would you think of the project if you were one of the many children whose Little League baseball field will be demolished? What would you think if you were one of their parents? How would you react to the project if you were a town official who had warm childhood memories of playing Little League baseball? Is there a national angle to the issue, and do other towns find themselves faced with the problem of trading playing fields for profits?

5. Divide broader topics into their component parts.

Consider whether the account of a specific news event involves a unique or newsworthy setting, interesting people to profile or a date that is significant for reasons beyond the event.

- Is a high school or college alumni gathering being hosted at a historically important site? Are several graduates of the class prominent in business or politics, or are some graduates teaching at the same institution from which they graduated? Is the reunion timed to coincide with a significant date, or is the date significant for any of the individual class members? How do current students view the reunion?
- Are any of the people identified in a hard news story involved in activities of note, aside from the reported incident? Does the setting have additional significance? Does the incident seem linked to another, earlier incident near or on the same date?

6. Pay attention to new and established local programs.

Watch for changes in the announced goals of programs or in the patterns of recruiting members and holding meetings.

- Are local seasonal programs continuing as in the past, or are changes being made in their focus and operation? Is this only a local trend, or is it national? Has your campus or town removed all religious symbols from Christmas displays? Is this happening in other nearby campuses or towns? Is this a national trend?
- Has the number of support group meetings announced in the local paper increased? How different are their goals from those of the past decade? How has the membership changed? Are these local or national trends?
- What is the status of the sororities and fraternities on campus? Are they more or less popular at other schools? Are they more or less popular than in earlier decades?

7. Read the personal and classified advertisements.

Local personal columns and classified advertisements reflect the nature and interests of the people and the area in which the newspaper is published.

- In the personal advertisements, are more men or more women advertising for partners? How do the proportions compare with the surrounding population? What are the advertisers telling about themselves and asking for in others? How do these advertisements compare with those placed in metropolitan newspapers?
- What are the most frequently advertised job opportunities in the classified advertisements? How do the positions differ from those of earlier years? What does this say about the local area? How do the opportunities differ from those advertised in another locale or nationally?

8. Review your "interesting article ideas" files.

Before you can consult files, you have to create them, so begin to save interesting articles in specifically identified file folders. The filing system does not have to be elaborate, but it should contain folders labeled with every possible topic in which you have some interest. As articles appear in magazines and newspapers, or as you write down details from television and radio reports and what others tell you, place the material into their subject folders. On days that you feel completely without article topic possibilities, read through the files to find angles on possible topics. Such files are also valuable to provide resources when you *do* have an idea but need names of sources and want background on a topic.

FOCUSING ON THE SUBJECT

Once you have an idea, or several ideas, collect information to determine whether the topic really is worthwhile and one that will keep *you* interested. A competent writer can write a good article about almost any topic. A writer who has an interest in the topic will write an even better article about it, and interest others in the topic, as well.

Where do you begin? Before writing any story, hard news or feature, create a focused statement that *succinctly* explains the point of the story and how it should be told. Those contests that ask entrants to describe their dream vacation, ideal date or perfect home in 50 words or less make a valuable point. The writer who cannot express the essence of a story within that word limit probably does not have a clear idea of the subject and will waste a lot of time in gathering unnecessary information. You should not ignore the importance of the focused statement, but take care that you do not make it too general. The following statements characterize an idea that grew out of a writer's attendance at a memorial service for the late American poet Allen Ginsberg. Notice how much more direction the second statement provides the potential writer.

Focused Statements

Statement 1: Many people mourned the death of poet Allen Ginsberg at memorial services throughout the country, and quite a few people were present at a recent memorial service held in Paterson, New Jersey, one sunny Sunday in early June of this year.

Statement 2: Of the many memorial services held in honor of poet Allen Ginsberg, none was more meaningful than that held by family members, friends and admirers on June 8, 1997, at the Great Falls in the poet's hometown of Paterson, New Jersey.

Look carefully at the two statements. Given only a cursory review, they appear to contain the same information, but Statement 2 reminds the article writer of several more specific points that will focus the gathering of information and the writing. Following that statement, the writer will 1) emphasize the special bond between the poet and Paterson, 2) identify family and friends present at the service, 3) relate the setting of the Great Falls to the poet's work and 4) describe the events of the day.

Once you have expressed the idea clearly, determine how much information is needed to write the story. Most writers have at least a core idea about their topics, gained from reading, knowledge and experience. If this is not the case for a given article, you will have to acquire that knowledge by doing some background research. Such research does not have to be extensive, but it should provide a general understanding of the subject. This is *not* a gathering of the information to be used directly in the specific story; that comes later. Instead, this foray into research is meant to acquaint you with the general subject area so that you can establish a context for the story.

What do you do if the assignment is to write an article about the memorial service for Allen Ginsberg, but you know very little about him or the people who will be present?

- At the least, you should read a good biographical sketch and skim through a bibliography of his works.
- Contact the organizers of the event and ask if you can obtain an advance copy of the program or a list of planned participants and activities.
- Review several of the subject's works to gain a feeling for the writing of the man being honored.
- Compile a list of the subject's newsworthy activities, much of which can be found in clippings files or a good biography, if one is available.

Armed with some background knowledge, you can now determine the value of the information you already have about the subject—and gain a better idea of the type and extent of the information that you have yet to collect.

A story about the memorial service can be either hard news or a feature article, depending on the manner of the assignment. How much information you need depends on the nature of the article.

Hard news article. If you are writing a hard news article, the piece will mainly require factual material. Therefore, you will need to obtain only a few facts beyond the background on the subject, the information provided by the program, and the on-site observations that occur.

Naturally, you would not even pretend to be ready to write a story based *only* on the background information and the program. Potential participants might become ill and cancel, rain might cause a postponement, activities might be added and other individuals might make last-minute appearances. The immediacy of the hard news article demands your presence at the event and an accurate record of all the facts.

Soft news or feature article. The feature article requires all of the details that you would gather for a hard news article. In addition, you are expected to record your observations and reactions to the event and the subject, as well as the reactions of others.

What do *you* know about the story? The best way to answer that question is to write a *framework* piece, nothing more than an outline in narrative form. Without notes, write down everything that you know about the specific story, taking care to use whatever details have been gathered through background research and from the source of the initial assignment. You may find that you know a lot more than you think—or a lot *less*. Either way, the framework piece provides a way of measuring how much and what type of information must be collected. It will also help you decide the means by which to collect that information.

Framework Piece
The Memorial Service for Allen Ginsberg
at the Great Falls, Paterson, New Jersey

A memorial service to honor American poet Allen Ginsberg will be held at the Great Falls, Paterson, New Jersey, on June 8, 1997. Ginsberg was a major figure in the antiwar effort during the Vietnam era, and he often appeared at protest demonstrations. He was considered a revolutionary figure, creating poetry that took a moral and social stand, but many literary critics and other members of society criticized his use of "vulgar" and "obscene" language. His raw images and open mention of sexual acts in the poems resulted in bans against his work. He was also a founding member of the Beat movement whose work, along with that of Jack Kerouac, Neil Cassady, William Burroughs, Gregory Corso and others, put a new face on literary expression. Born into the Jewish faith, Ginsberg became a devout Buddhist as an adult. His father, Louis, who died in 1976, was an English teacher in the Paterson school system for many years. His mother, Naomi, who died in 1956, was the subject of several of his poems. His 96-year-old stepmother, Edith, is expected to be present at the service.

Your framework piece can be substantially longer and more detailed, depending on the topic and on the nature of the article you are writing. A newspaper article, either hard news or feature, is usually assigned, and the editor will frequently provide restrictions and requirements for the piece. If the feature article is self-generated, you must not only initiate the ideas but also remain open to the possibilities that exist for any given topic. In short, do not approach a subject with rigidly determined, preconceived ideas. Allow the data that you collect to shape the eventual writing, and be ready to expand or delete ideas.

THE QUERY LETTER

Assigned articles are often accompanied by an editor's directions, but most magazine articles are self-generated by freelance writers or regular contributors who find a topic and suggest that editors let them write about it. Some magazines ask that a freelance writer write the article in advance and then send a completed copy on speculation. If the work is suitable to their readers' interests, and if it is otherwise well written, the writer receives an offer at the magazine's standard rate, calculated on either a per-word basis or a flat fee for a specified word-length range.

Many more magazines do not have the needed staff to read through articles, so they require that writers send a *query letter* first. If the editor likes the topic and the sound of the query letter, the writer will then be asked to send the article for editorial review, with no promise by the magazine to purchase the piece. After a writer has sold several articles to a publication, some magazines will respond to the query letter with a contract that authorizes the writer to complete the piece and promises to pay a "kill fee." The kill fee, usually worth from 15 to 25 percent of the proposed payment for the article, is paid if the magazine accepts the work and then has to cancel its publication for any reason.

Do a little advance work before sending a query letter to an editor. Following are several tips to guide you:

1. Before submitting a query letter, become familiar with the audience and content of the magazine by reading through several recent past issues. Each publication has a separate personality, determined by its audience.

2. Consult the masthead of the chosen magazine or refer to *Writer's Market*, found in the reference section of most public and academic libraries, to obtain the name of a specific editor to whom you can direct the manuscript. Do not be surprised if the selected publication directs writers to simply submit their work to "The Nonfiction Editor." *THE NEW YORKER* is among publications that refuse to provide a specific name, even when a writer calls for that information.

3. Construct a query letter that speaks to the specific magazine audience, and expect that the eventual article will have to meet the same requirement. The character and style of a magazine are shaped by its readers and advertisers, and the writing must be consistent with both.

Following is a query letter for an article about the memorial service for Allen Ginsberg. It is somewhat more detailed than most writers might use for an event still in the future, or a subject who has not yet been interviewed, but it contains the elements of all good query letters.

Sample Query Letter

Nonfiction Editor
THE NEW YORKER
20 West 43rd Street
New York, NY 10036-7441

To the Nonfiction Editor:

Poet Allen Ginsberg was an American icon whose influence went far beyond the literary world. As a founder of the Beat movement in the 1950s and an antiwar activist in the 1960s and early 1970s, he combined a passion for social change with his love of the spoken word to shake the foundations of traditional society. Many who lived through those decades remember newspaper photographs of a long-haired, full-bearded bear of a man passing out flowers and reciting poetry as National Guardsmen and police brandished rifles to disperse the crowds. In later years, he practiced faithfully his Buddhist faith and taught at Brooklyn College, where he shared his love of poetry and life with eager students.

I had the good fortune of meeting Allen (as he asked everyone to call him) several times when he read at Montclair State University, when it was still only a college and I was still only a student. He remembered the experience of reading there, for mention of the college appears in one of his last poems, "Death and Fame," written on February 22, 1997, and published in the April 21, 1997, issue of *THE NEW YORKER.* He would not remember me, of course, for I was only one of many anonymous students granted the honor of speaking with him afterward, although at that long-ago meeting he did turn a phrase regarding a connection between my first name and "sunshine."

After his death on April 5, 1997, many memorial readings and services were held throughout the nation, but none could be more significant than that which took place on June 8, 1997, at the Great Falls in Paterson, New Jersey, his hometown. Officials initially resisted the event, recalling Allen's admission to illegal behavior and near conviction two decades before, but they eventually relented. And, as he predicted, almost everyone whom he named in "Death & Fame" appeared, supplemented by a United States Congressman and several councilmen.

Would you be interested in an approximately 4,000-word article, entitled "Celebrating Allen," that recounts the events and reactions of that day? The participants were varied, and one councilman was even moved to bring flowers, some of which he passed out to the crowd before throwing the bulk of them over a bridge and "liberating" them into the rushing river far below.

I look forward to your response, and I enclose a stamped, self-addressed envelope for your convenience.

Sincerely,

Dawn B. Sova

Chapter Two

Gathering Information

A newspaper or magazine article is only as good as its weakest source of information. Most people believe much of what they read; thus, the negative consequences of inadvertently incorporating false or misleading information into an article can be far-reaching. As the writer, you are accountable for what appears under your byline, even errors in information given by a presumed expert, or falsehoods provided by a subject in an interview. As a result, you *must* be careful in checking facts, judicious in selecting your sources and meticulous in reporting your observations. That may appear to be a tall order, but it really is not—*if* you take the time to carefully scrutinize your sources of information.

The main ways of gathering information include observation, interviews, background research and on-site document research. Rarely is an article derived from only one of these sources, and most articles depend on a combination or two of more of them.

FACT VERSUS OPINION

Before collecting information, become familiar with the differences between fact and opinion. A hard news story usually contains mostly facts. What people think about a newsworthy situation or incident is important only if the individuals offering opinions are prominent in the action. Unfortunately for the writer, these people often refuse to speak with the press.

The feature, or soft news, article is more likely to contain opinions, but the writer has to be as careful in questioning the sources of those opinions as in scrutinizing facts.

What is the difference between a fact and an opinion? A *fact* is information that you can check and determine to be correct or incorrect. An *opinion* is simply one's views regarding an issue. Before gathering information, make certain that you know the difference—and that you identify the difference in your notes.

Facts. People have a tendency to present what are really opinions as statements of fact. Remember that a fact can be proved to be correct or incorrect in several ways:

- Through personal observation
- By examining records
- By reviewing statistics
- By comparison with another person's observation

Any information, whether true or false, is a fact if it can be proved or disproved. Review the following statements:

A. Women in the United States currently enjoy a higher average income than men.
B. Cats are more popular than dogs as pets in the United States.
C. More than half the students in Everytown High School are illiterate.
D. Dr. Friendly says that we can live in harmony.

All four statements are facts. You may question their accuracy, but they *can* be proved correct or incorrect:

1. The accuracy of Statement A can be verified by obtaining U.S. Department of Labor data related to income for men and women.
2. Statement B may seem like an opinion, but it can be proved true or false by using pet ownership survey data.
3. Although Statement C seems to be someone's disgruntled opinion, illiteracy is a defined condition, and proving the fact just requires assessing the number of students who meet or fail to meet the requirements of the condition.

4. Finally, that we can live in harmony is an opinion held by Dr. Friendly, *but* whether he actually makes this assertion is a fact that can be checked by asking him. When using a fact such as Statement D, be careful to include the name of your source.

Opinions. Interpretations in hard news stories should be left to the readers, not expressed by the writer. When opinions are included, they should be clearly labeled as such, and the source of the opinion should be identified. Feature stories usually call for opinions, but the same care must be taken to play fair with the reader. Opinions consist of personal viewpoints, so they cannot be proved or disproved. However, the extent to which an opinion is valid can be assessed in several ways:

- By determining the reliability of the person offering the opinion
- By examining the data on which the opinion is based
- By ascertaining the authority of the person expressing the opinion

Opinions can be hard to assess, so the careful writer *always* identifies the source within the article.

A. Dr. Everyman, dean of students, views students in the 1990s as better prepared for college than those of earlier decades.
B. The attending physician characterized the fugitive as extremely attractive to women.
C. The quality of education in Everytown is very low.

Such opinions can add reader interest, but the source may need to be explained further.

1. Statement A seems to be a reasonably expressed opinion, given the position of the speaker. The problem lies in his ability to express a valid opinion that relates to earlier decades. Has he held a similar position or the same position during the earlier decades? If so, then no one will question his ability to comment on earlier decades. If, however, Dr. Everyman has recently become a dean of students and has worked in student personnel administration only in the 1990s, he has no experience on which to base his comparison. If you *must* use his opinion and cannot find a more experienced individual, clearly

indicate in the article that he is expressing an opinion based on hearsay or research.

2. Statement B *may* be a valid opinion if the attending physician has observed the fugitive interacting with women or if the attending physician is a woman. If either case applies, the writer should include that information. If neither case applies, then further explanation is needed to support the validity of the opinion. What qualifies the "attending physician" to come to such a conclusion? How valid is such a conclusion?

3. Statement C appears to be the opinion of the writer, because no attribution is given and no appeal is made to authority, to statistics or to a reliable source. A statement of this type leaves a writer open to extensive criticism and requires more information to support the assertion. To place so generalized a statement in an article is more than careless; it is irresponsible.

The ability to discern the difference between fact and opinion is important in information gathering. You will save time by starting out smart, thus reducing the amount of checking and rechecking required and ensuring that articles are accurate and well supported.

OBSERVATION

Observation skills are important in writing both hard news and feature stories. You must leave personal opinion out of hard news stories, but the inclusion of descriptive details based on your observations is vital in bringing a story to life and providing readers with a sense of immediacy. The benefit of a writer's observations is that they eliminate the need to rely on possible inaccuracies in the reports of others regarding an occurrence. At the same time, a greater burden is placed on you to re-create the scene and the players.

What kind of information can your observations provide? Consider a story about a student demonstration that occurs in front of the college administration building to protest a state-mandated increase of tuition. You might observe the following:

- Number of demonstrators
- Distribution of ages (freshmen, seniors and graduate students) of those protesting
- Appearance and content of the posters and signs
- Behavior of the protesters
- Responses of authorities
- Nature of the surroundings
- Weather
- Changes in protesters' enthusiasm levels over time
- Nature of verbal exchanges between the protesters and observers or law enforcement officials

Don't restrict your observations to your perspective as a reporter. Instead, role-play as you observe, and attempt to experience the situation from the perspectives of the students, the administration and the security personnel, as well. You may not find much of this material directly usable in a hard news article because it is actually supposition, but the different perspective will sharpen your own observations and view of the facts. You will also find that such role-playing is effective in helping you to formulate questions that will result in more valuable quotations from those whom you interview.

INTERVIEWS

A well-planned interview is a good source of information, which can provide the writer with opinions, quotations, observations and facts. This information, however, can be either very accurate and valuable or very inaccurate and damaging to the writer's article, credibility and career. Therefore, the subject of the interview must be carefully selected, and the interview must be carefully planned, or nothing of value will emerge.

Whom do you select to interview? The topic and nature of the article determine who can provide the most valuable information to supplement other means of information gathering.

- An article covering a crime may be enriched by an interview with an observer, an innocent bystander, the victim, the victim's family or a law enforcement official, depending on the focus of your article.
- The article about a student demonstration on a college campus may benefit from an interview with one of the protesters, the college president, the parent of a protester or state officials who passed the tuition increase.
- A feature article that profiles an individual is usually based in part on an interview with the person and benefits from interviews with both admirers and critics.

The interviewer's approach is as important to the success of the interview as choosing the right interview subject. A good interviewer has to be a good listener who can set the subject at ease. You have to approach the person with sensitivity and recognize that some issues will be difficult to discuss. You also have to be prepared to listen carefully and to watch the individual's body language as you ask various questions. Observe what an individual doesn't say or doesn't respond to, because what is omitted can be just as revealing as the responses.

Before scheduling an interview, research the background of your interview subject. Do not embarrass yourself by asking basic factual questions if answers to these can be found in clippings, public records, previously published interviews or press releases. If you can do so without offending your subject, speak with people who are familiar with the person so that you can gain other perspectives about personality and quirks. Then determine your aim for the interview so that you can provide your subject with an idea of the direction your questions will take. Busy individuals, who will not want to be faced with a barrage of questions that might consume hours of their time, are more likely to agree to meet with you if they are familiar with your proposed boundaries. You don't have to supply the interview schedule, but you should provide the subject with the angle or approach that you intend to take.

Plan the questions that you will ask before you schedule the interview. You cannot possibly ask everything that is on your mind, so narrow your questions to those that will elicit the most important information for your purpose. Identify the crucial information first and create questions to request that information; then create secondary questions to hold in reserve for use as the interview progresses. If the session goes well, you might have the opportunity to ask all of your questions. If it doesn't, you will at least be prepared to elicit the crucial information.

Begin with the least-threatening questions, usually factual, before moving to those that might put the subject on the spot. Following are several types of questions with examples of how you might phrase them if you interviewed a college administrator for the student demonstration story, which was used as an example in the discussion of observation.

• Background questions that elicit the history of an issue

Example:

> When was the last time that students at the college demonstrated against the administration? What was the issue then? How effective were they in achieving their goals?

• Questions that trace the evolution of an issue

Example:

> When did the administration first learn of the students' intention to demonstrate? What have student representatives stated as their goals? What has been the communication with the governor's office regarding student demands?

• Clarification questions that require the subject to explain or define terms that relate to the issue

Example:

> How much more tuition will the average student at this university pay? How is the increase going to be assessed? What is the present average cost per semester for a student?

• Questions that ask the subject to verify information, both for accuracy and to elicit quotations

Example:

> How many students currently attend the university? What is the size of the average freshman class? What can you tell me about the demographic breakdown of the student population?

- Questions that ask the subject to react through the eyes of others involved with the issue

Example:

> What differences will this increase in state university tuition make in the choices of college-bound high school seniors? What type of modification in thinking will your financial aid officers have to undergo? How will the parents of most of your students cope with this increase?

- Questions that project events into the future

Example:

> How will this increase affect enrollment for next fall? Does the university anticipate a decrease in services in any areas? How will the demographics of the student population change?

- Questions that identify comments made by others and ask the subject to react

Example:

> The governor has stated the following: "A $2,000 per year increase in tuition for the state university is not unreasonable when we compare it to the high tuition costs at Ivy League universities." How do you respond to the governor's statement?

- Open-ended questions that allow the subject to add anything to the interview that you may have failed to ask

Example:

> What about the issues have I ignored?

The way in which you conduct *yourself* is as important as the way in which you conduct the interview. The interview will be more successful if you do more than simply ask questions and record the answers.

Treat the interview subject as you would anyone in whom you have an interest.

1. Pay attention to the answer that the subject is giving to the present question and resist the temptation to think about the next question.
2. Create a transition between the questions to maintain the train of thought and to provide an illusion of conversation.
3. Show interest in the subject by making eye contact, nodding your head, murmuring agreement, asking for brief explanations and showing other encouragement.
4. Resist the urge to put your two cents' worth into the interview responses.
5. Remain flexible regarding the direction of the interview, and be ready to follow an interesting thread of discussion that does not exist in your list of interview questions.

Above all, you must control the interview and the direction of the questions, but never forget that you are dealing with another human being who has *agreed* to speak with you. Be courteous, be sensitive and, when the moment is right, be quiet and let the subject talk.

BACKGROUND RESEARCH

Background research used to mean research in the public library or in newspaper reference files, but the definition has expanded. Widespread use of the computer has added another source of background research— electronic databases, most of which are based on material that can still be found in print form in many libraries. A mix of the two sources can be useful to provide information for writing articles for newspapers and magazines.

The value of the library for obtaining background information depends on the subject of your research and the type of library that you consult. College and university libraries may contain extensive legal reference material, government documents, transcripts of congressional hearings and court cases, government reports, national newspapers and telephone directories. Public libraries, as well as college and university libraries, contain reference materials such as almanacs; encyclopedias; books containing financial ratings and names of top executives of corporations; and a range of magazines in print, microfilm and microfiche. Public libraries also carry local telephone directories and newspapers, many now stored in databases and going back several years.

The library may also provide quick access to online research sources, as many structures formerly called "libraries" have now changed their designation to "media centers." Using public access, you may be able to log on to a range of data sources, including government census information, magazine abstracts and updates of the status of bills under consideration by Congress. Thousands of "bulletin boards" and discussion groups exist that are dedicated to specific topics, and these can be useful in finding experts in a given area. One caution, however, is that you have to assess carefully the validity of the source and not depend too strongly on an e-mail message or an opinion expressed spontaneously. Be skeptical and apply the same strenuous standards to such information as you would to a face-to-face interview.

ON-SITE RECORDS RESEARCH

Public records contain a substantial amount of valuable information about people and institutions, but the access to such records varies widely from jurisdiction to jurisdiction. Many people mistakenly believe that The Freedom of Information Act has made all public documents available, but the Act applies only to *federal* documents. Further, some federal documents are limited by exemptions; among these are records related to law enforcement investigations, critical foreign policy or national defense issues, and internal policy or personnel issues.

On a local level, you might consult records of the following to obtain information for stories:

Building inspection information and housing permits
City council meetings minutes
City expenses

Corporate expenses and management
Court filings and trial transcripts
County expenses
Fire department activities
Fish and game licensing
Military service
Motor vehicle registration
Personal property loans
Police arrests
Property taxes
Public works projects and expenses
Real estate transactions
School district activities and expenses
Voter registration information

How can you make use of these records in an article? Consult several of these sources, and you will be surprised by how much information they provide about people.

What if you choose to explore the safety of the dormitories on campus? The campus administration may refuse to cooperate or claim that no information is available. That should not deter you. You can examine the records of the fire department in the municipality in which the campus is located to determine the frequency and results of fire inspections, the records of fire alarms, and the number of calls in a given period, including response times. The office of the municipal building inspector contains records that reveal whether the college has been cited for building code violations, as well as information regarding all permits that have been issued for new construction and improvements. Take into account that some college campuses may sprawl over more than one municipality, and be careful to identify the location of buildings.

A reporter who wants to explore the background of a politician running for local, county or state office can find substantial information about the candidate in public records. *Building inspection and housing permit records* will expose how the individual maintains any commercial properties owned. *City expense records* will show how a former city official carried out duties, and *city council meeting records* reveal resolutions and ordinances that the individual supported. *Court records* provide information on criminal and civil cases in which the individual might be involved, and *police records* indicate the existence of criminal offenses. Finally, *real estate records* provide information about deeds for property owned by the individual and the annual taxes.

The information-gathering phase of writing articles for newspapers and magazines is pure drudgery. You track down sources, check facts, follow numerous leads and compile stacks of notes. Many leads may produce nothing important, and much information may have to be filed away to be used in another story. If you have been careful in this stage, the next step is to begin writing the story.

Chapter Three

Writing the Effective Article Lead

The most important paragraph in an article is the lead, the first paragraph of a hard news story and the first several paragraphs of a feature. Lose readers at this point, and you have lost them for good.

Think of the lead as a personal sales pitch designed to lure readers into your story and to give them a clear idea of the rest of the article. The impact on readers has to be immediate in a hard news article. In a soft news or feature article, you can take longer to present the main point. In short, the nature of the information—its significance and immediacy—determines the type of lead to use.

Either way, before investing too much time in your prose, readers should know the *who, what, when, where, why* and *how* of the story early in their reading. Answer these six questions of journalists, and readers will turn repeatedly to stories appearing under your byline. Of course, you must also keep any promises that you make in the lead to supply further information in the body of the story.

THE HARD NEWS LEAD

Significant news stories—such as those recounting natural or man-made disasters, national crises, breaking news (local, national or international), the passage of major legislation, violent death or the death of a well-known individual—require the hard news lead. To be news, the event must have just occurred, will soon occur or is occurring, so only the day, not the date, need be identified.

The approach is a vital element in the *inverted pyramid* news story form. Although many feature writers may criticize the approach, feeling that the old reason for the form has passed, most newspapers continue to structure their hard news stories in this way.

Simply put, the inverted pyramid starts with a lead sentence or paragraph that clearly presents the most significant information of the story, the 5 Ws + H. From that point, information in the story appears in descending order of importance, in paragraphs that support the lead with details and evidence. The least important information appears at the bottom of the story.

The form developed for a very practical reason nearly a century ago, when type was still set by hand. Cutting a story could be a grueling task for editors and typesetters if key information were scattered throughout the text. The inverted pyramid form is efficient because an editor can simply remove paragraphs at the bottom of the story to fit column space without losing vital information or wasting time in restructuring.

Despite many technical advances, today's fast-paced society makes the inverted-pyramid form even more relevant in retaining readers than in earlier years. Most contemporary newspaper readers do not enjoy the news at leisure. Instead, they scan the paper, taking only the time necessary to read the headlines and the first few sentences of stories. Indoctrinated to receiving condensed news through radio and television, they do not have the patience to wade through a lot of description to get to the point of a story. Your job is to make certain that essential information appears at the beginning.

The Summary Lead

The hard news lead can take several forms, the most common being the *summary lead,* which provides the answers to all six questions of journalists in one compact sentence, or two at most. Not only must the writer pack a lot of information into a brief space, but that space must also identify succinctly and clearly all of the elements of the story. The opening must also be strong and dynamic to capture readers' attention immediately. The writer can accomplish this goal by using active rather than passive voice, in order to emphasize the action of the incident.

Before attempting to write the lead, sort out the details for yourself by listing briefly the answers to the questions that frame the story. You will find that providing the responses to these questions is the most concise way in which to describe any occurrence. Then write a sentence of approximately 30 words and include all six responses: who, what, when, where, why and how. You can keep the word count down by eliminating decorative clauses, phrases and descriptive words. "Just the facts" is the rule at this point.

To observe how a writer can turn the basic facts of a story into a solid summary lead, consider the sketchy information provided in the student demonstration story that serves as an example for gathering information in Chapter Two. We can provide responses to each of the questions and add to the information, if necessary, to supply material for the lead.

Who: College students
What: A protest
When: Noon on Wednesday, April 16, 1998
Where: Student union building at Montcalm State University
Why: State-mandated tuition hike for the state colleges of New Jersey
How: Demonstration and blocking entrance to a building

The order in which you combine this information in a summary lead is not prescribed by any journalistic rules. Sometimes *who* is more important than *where*; *when* might be more important than *what*; *why* or *how* might overshadow everything else. Each incident imposes its own structure on the order in which information appears in the lead.

The summary leads of many stories open with the grammatical form of the simple sentence, subject-verb-object, to tell readers *who* performed the action(s), *what* action was performed and *who* received the result of the action. *Where* and *when* the action occurred are then related, followed by a brief indication of *why* or *how* the action occurred. The order is sometimes reversed. A writer has to decide which piece of information among the six questions of journalists is most important, and then place that information first in the lead. Consider the following manipulations of the details related to the student demonstration.

Summary Lead 1—Emphasis on "Who"

Students at Montcalm State University demonstrated by carrying signs and blocking the entrance to the student union building on Wednesday to protest a state-mandated tuition increase scheduled to take effect in September 1998.

Summary Lead 2—Emphasis on "What"

A protest against the state-mandated tuition increase scheduled to take effect in September 1998 was staged on Wednesday at Montcalm State University by students who demonstrated by carrying signs and blocking the entrance to the student union building.

Summary Lead 3—Emphasis on "When"

On Wednesday, students at Montcalm State University demonstrated by carrying signs and blocking the entrance to the student union building to protest the state-mandated tuition increase scheduled to take effect in September 1998.

Summary Lead 4—Emphasis on "Where"

At Montcalm State University on Wednesday, students protested the state-mandated tuition increase, scheduled to take effect in September 1998, by demonstrating with signs and blocking the entrance to the student union building.

Summary Lead 5—Emphasis on "Why"

To protest the state-mandated tuition increase scheduled to take effect on September 1998, students at Montcalm State University demonstrated by carrying signs on Wednesday and blocking the entrance to the student union building.

Summary Lead 6—Emphasis on "How"

By demonstrating with signs and blocking the entrance to the student union building on Wednesday, students at Montcalm State University staged a protest against the state-mandated tuition increase scheduled to take effect on September 1998.

The different arrangements of the same basic information results in more than one informative lead. Each example emphasizes a different element of the topic, telling a reader that the article following the given lead will emphasize a different facet of the topic. Thus, the article following Summary Lead 1 should focus largely on the students; the one following Summary Lead 2 should be more concerned with the protest; the one developing from Summary Lead 3 will emphasize the timing of the protest; the one developing from Summary Lead 4 will deal significantly with the Montcalm State University campus; the one following Summary Lead 5 will be concerned with the state-mandated tuition increase; and the one following Summary Lead 6 will relate the actions used by the students in demonstrating and blocking the building entrance.

Observe that all but one of the summary lead examples use active voice verbs. The one lead that employs the passive voice (Summary Lead 2) places emphasis on the action of the demonstration rather than on the actors (the students), the location (Montcalm State University), the time (Wednesday), the reason (to protest the tuition increase) or their means of protesting (demonstrating and blocking the entrance to the student union building).

What effect does the passive voice have in that lead? How would a change from the active to the passive voice change the impact of the other leads? Would any *not* change?

When writing summary leads for hard news articles, ask how your choice of emphasis and voice changes the intention of the article.

- How will readers react to the lead?
- What have you promised readers? What should they expect in the rest of the article?
- Where do *you* want emphasis to lie in the article?
- Where does the lead promise readers that the emphasis will lie?
- Are the lead and the story structured to appeal to your readers?

The final question is important because the market in which the hard news article appears also influences the information required in the summary lead to attract readers. People focus on different concerns when reading a campus newspaper, as opposed to a local weekly or daily paper or a regional or national daily paper. For this reason, the generic summary lead examples need the addition of more specific information if they are going to appeal to a campus or local readership.

- Who *specifically* protested? Undergraduate or graduate students? Both?
- Was the protest led by a specific group? The student government officers and representatives? A specific student committee? A specific student leader?
- What is the name of the student union building?
- How much is the tuition increase? In percentage? In dollars?

Include more specific identification of people and places when a locally breaking story is published close to home. Readers outside the region have little interest in the names of unknown individuals, but readers near the occurrence often know those involved. Thus, Summary Lead 1 might be revised as follows to appeal to a campus audience:

> **Graduate** students led by **James Johns** at Montcalm State University demonstrated and blocked the entrance to **Triphammer Hall** on Wednesday to protest a state-mandated **25%** tuition increase scheduled to take effect in September 1998.

The extent to which specific information should be included in a summary lead depends on the intended readership. Readers having no connection to the university campus would not have any idea that Triphammer Hall is the student union building, so the type of structure rather than the name should appear in the summary lead of an article published in a regional paper. The name of the leader is meaningless to regional leaders, so the name need not appear so early in the lead. If an article about the protest appears in a regional or national paper, the state mandating the increase must certainly be identified, although it may not appear in a story published in a campus or local paper.

Variations on the Hard News Lead

Even within the seemingly narrow confines of the summary lead, writers can include variations. Depending on the story, *attribution, quotations* and *identification of impact* are all viable alternatives.

Attribution in the hard news lead. The attribution lead must be used when the information for the article has come from a source other than the eyewitness account of the reporter. More of a protection for your reputation for accuracy than a stylistic technique, this type of lead is effective only if the individual to whom you attribute the information is significant.

Compare the effect of the following two accounts. Which one would you trust more?

Example:

University president Aaron Christian told reporters that students demonstrated and blocked the entrance to the student union building on Wednesday to protest the 25% state-mandated tuition increase scheduled to take effect in September 1998.

Example:

Graduate student James Johns told reporters that students demonstrated and blocked the entrance to the student union building at Montcalm State University on Wednesday to protest the 25% state-mandated tuition increase scheduled to take effect in September 1998.

Quotations in the hard news lead. The limited word count of the hard news lead requires that only significant quotations conveying relevant information and opinions are included. A further consideration to make the most of the lead is that you should use a quotation spoken only by an individual involved in the story or by someone who is important. This caution is similar to your choice in attributions.

Both speakers are involved in the incident, but consider which of the two quotations and speakers are more significant.

Example:

"Many students will be adversely affected by the 25% state-mandated tuition increase," stated Montcalm State University president Aaron Christian, who supported the Wednesday protest during which students demonstrated and blocked the entrance to the student union building.

Example:

"This is the first real issue we've had," reported Montcalm State University graduate student James Johns and a leader of the Wednesday protest of the state-mandated 25% tuition increase during which students demonstrated and blocked the entrance to the student union building.

Identification of impact in the hard news lead. To add reader relevance to a story, writers often incorporate the "so what?" element to the hard news lead. If a story will have impact on their lives, readers are more likely to consider it important and to read it. Impact can be indicated in several ways.

Reread the first example of a lead using a quotation from Montcalm State University president Aaron Christian. Incorporated in his statement is an indication of the impact that the increase will have on MSU students. Other impact might be included in different leads, including how the change will impact parents of students who attend state colleges, the university enrollment or students of specific demographic backgrounds.

Consider how Summary Lead 1 is enhanced by indicating the impact of the situation:

> Students at Montcalm State University demonstrated by carrying signs and blocking the entrance to the student union building to protest a state-mandated tuition increase, scheduled to take effect in September 1998 and **expected to prevent many from returning to school.**

THE SOFT NEWS OR FEATURE LEAD

The feature article aims to do more than to inform the reader. In the effort to evoke a reaction and to elicit human emotion, the feature writer takes a longer time to introduce all of the elements to the reader. Feature leads offer substantially more variety than leads that are part of the inverted pyramid structure. Soft news or feature articles vary greatly in length, as do their leads. Unlike the length-limited hard news leads, feature leads can be several paragraphs in length, assigning one or two of the answers to the 5 Ws + H to an entire paragraph, and include substantial detail.

Among the variations of the feature lead are those that begin with an *anecdote*, a *quotation*, a *description*, a *teasing pun or double entendre*, or an *extended summary*. Many feature leads, however, combine elements from several of the five types.

The Anecdotal Lead
The brief story contained in an anecdotal lead should reflect the larger story of the feature article, drawing the reader into the drama, conflict,

tragedy or joy that the article develops further. The writer may choose to engage the reader's sympathy, to establish a mood or to provide an example of the discussion that will follow.

The following anecdote appears in the lead of a lengthy (4,000-word) article that cautions people to be wary of telephone solicitors and provides readers with information for avoiding being defrauded.

Twelve years ago, I was desperate for a job to help me through college. The campus paper usually carried a good number of ads soliciting college students to work as telemarketers, promising "High commissions. Make $$$$. Work your own hours. Steady income."

What did they want me to do? Sell magazine subscriptions? Contract for chimney cleaning? Make appointments for home repairs?

I called a number in one of the ads and made an appointment for an interview at their office, located within walking distance of the campus. With high spirits, I strolled to the interview, walked confidently into the office and filled out a lengthy application given to me by the receptionist. A few minutes after disappearing through another door with my application, she emerged and told me to go in.

"Mr. Smith will interview you now."

"Mr. Smith" looked pleasant enough. He greeted me and shuffled papers on his desk as he spoke to me. He told me that my calls would be "important" and that I would earn a 15% commission on everything that I sold, but he had to be sure that I could read the "script" with the "proper emotion." Then he thrust several sheets into my hand and told me to read, and I did.

"Good morning (afternoon/evening), Mr. (Mrs.) _____. You don't know me, but thanks to good people like you, people stuck in a wheelchair, like me, have a lot to be thankful for. Here at the _____ Shelter, we produce a lot of fine products that we sell to keep ourselves self-sufficient. . . ."

The anecdote is clear in showing that the writer, who can stroll blithely to the interview and walk confidently into the office, was expected to lie to the people about her physical condition. She was also expected to claim that she was disabled and a member of a shelter that produces the goods that she is hawking by telephone. The clear falseness of the situation, and the prospect that her potential employer was defrauding a vulnerable group, the disabled, as well as potential customers, arouses indignation in readers who are now ready to read the rest of the article about other fraudulent telemarketing schemes.

The Quotation Lead

The use of a brief monologue, supported by additional narrative, is one of the easiest ways to gain the reader's interest quickly. Quotations should not be lengthy or boring. Short, even shocking, statements punctuated by terse explanatory narrative material work best to excite reader interest and to create the desired tone that will convince readers to go on.

The following quotations appear in the lead of a feature article that offers advice to mothers for getting along with their teenage daughters.

"What did you do to your hair?" Her mother's voice rose to a shrill pitch. "How could you chop it off like that? And your skirts. So short! People are going to think that you are wild!"

As the mother pursed her lips and shook her head in disapproval, her daughter rolled her eyes skyward and muttered, "You're old-fashioned."

The two glared at each other. Then my grandmother, the "flapper" with her "bobbed hair" and short skirts, left for her job. The year was 1923.

The words may be different, but three-quarters of a century later, mothers and daughters continue to enact similar scenes.

The quotations used are close enough to contemporary tone and content to arouse recognition in the modern reader. The accusations may be expressed in somewhat stilted language, but the reader doesn't notice this because the content draws attention away from the words used. Not until the writer chooses to explain the brief scene does the reader realize that this example of a "generation gap" is more than seven decades past. Instead of directly indicating the purpose of the article to follow, the writer allows the brief dialogue and supportive narrative to reveal the intention.

The Description Lead

The description of the person, place or occurrence that serves as the lead to a feature article has a weighty task. Instead of being a mere example to support the focus of the article, the description must be well chosen to symbolize the entire story. The most effective description moves quickly, using a combination of literary devices to capture the reader's ear as well as eye. To interest readers and to enhance the impact of the lead, include vivid detail and graphic imagery.

The following description serves as the lead for a feature article that examines the growing concern with random violence in contemporary society:

He has a black belt in karate and has trained in several other martial arts. His home is protected by an electronic surveillance system, and his children are trained never to give personal information to callers or strangers on the street. He always keeps his cars in perfect running order. Each member of his family carries a cellular phone at all times, to call for help in case of emergencies. He owns two registered handguns, one placed securely by his bedside and the other in a specially designed compartment under the driver's seat of his car.

Today, Joseph Andrews is in the intensive care ward of Metropolitan Hospital, the victim of multiple stab wounds after being attacked while he walked from his car to the office. The knife-wielding attacker surprised Mr. Andrews from behind, stabbing him in the neck and disabling him before he could put up a defense.

The description provides readers with an account of the many ways in which the victim has attempted to prepare for violence in society, from learning how to personally protect himself to protecting his family and his home. Using a matter-of-fact, unemotional tone to describe his preparation, the writer lulls the reader into complacency, then shatters that complacency in the second paragraph of the description. Despite all of his preparation and planning, Joseph Andrews also becomes a victim in a society in which the plague of random violence has claimed too many victims.

To be effective as a lead, this description must clearly reflect the writer's intention of examining the growing concern with this issue. This is *not* a "how-to" article that advises readers how to be safety conscious, nor is it an article that suggests ways in which readers can protect themselves against violence. Rather, the contrast between the victim's preparedness and his fate underscores the writer's view that the solutions lie far beyond the scope of individual defense against the violence. The article focuses on the social problem, after *showing*—not telling—that even the most defensive of individuals does not stand a chance against someone who is determined to commit a violent act.

The Teasing Pun or Double-Entendre Lead
The teasing pun or double-entendre leads are sometimes less successful than the more straightforward leads. The reason is that they depend on readers' familiarity with clichés, idiomatic expressions and "trendy" sayings that may no longer be current. Consider a well-known (to some) aphorism taken from Benjamin Franklin's *Poor Richard's Almanac,* one that has been used freely to caution against wasteful spending. Take a look at the following lead for a feature article that examines the manner in which government spending has increased the burdens on taxpayers in recent decades:

> A penny saved is a penny earned, or at least it used to be. Today, depending on how much money you make, that might be four-fifths, three-quarters or two-thirds of a penny earned, with the rest going to the government to pay your federal income tax. A penny, like everything else today, isn't what it used to be.

The lead fails to catch the reader's attention as fully if the phrase is unfamiliar, or if the reader has never heard the phrase offered as a serious precaution against overspending. After the statement and the disclaimer, the writer then sets up the discussion of the article by separating the different tax brackets into portions of that penny. To extend the use of the saying further into the body of the article would subject the writer to a charge of forsaking information for cleverness, so the lead completes the analogy and then allows the writer to move directly into a discussion of the issue in the next paragraph.

The Extended Summary Lead

The extended summary lead is simply a longer and more detailed version of the summary lead used in writing the hard news article. Each of the six questions of journalists—who, what, when, where, why, and how—is developed into several sentences, one or two questions per paragraph. Instead of attempting to combine all of the basic information into one sentence, the writer has the leisure to develop the mood and the ideas that will later be scrutinized in the body of the article. This lead should be reserved for longer articles that can bear the weight of the greater length.

The key to selecting the current lead style lies in determining the tone as well as the information that you want to convey to your readers. The right beginning will draw readers to an article, hooking them and making them stay until they have finished every paragraph. The wrong beginning will leave you writing for yourself—ultimately a very unsatisfying experience.

Chapter Four

Building an Effective Foundation

Good ideas require good writing to create an article that keeps readers interested beyond the lead. Well-constructed sentences and strong paragraph organization, along with correct grammar, usage and spelling, produce effective copy.

Why pay attention to these details? Many writers mistakenly believe that they have to focus only on ideas, leaving the expression of those ideas, including grammar and spelling, to the copy editors. Good copy editors are hard to come by, and, while they do correct such errors, a writer should not become lazy or sloppy and leave the rewriting of sentences and the paragraphing of prose to someone else. The article is under your byline, so make it yours entirely.

The same precaution is true in matters of grammar. Even if your writing experience is limited, you know that changing word order in a sentence, adding a comma or substituting one word for another also changes the meaning in a sentence. Copy editors are careful in their work, but they should not be forced into making major concept decisions in your writing.

WRITING EFFECTIVE SENTENCES

Simple sentences are still the best way to express your thoughts in an article. Layering on adjectives, adverbs, phrases and clauses may seem to be your way of showing erudition, but your show of learning is meaningless if no one reads your work. That does not mean that your writing will consist only of skeletal statements. Rather, your words must be well chosen, expressive and consistent with the tone of the article topic. Your sentences must clearly say what they mean without making the reader labor through needless description or jargon.

The basic building block of article structure is the sentence. Created with care, sentences provide strong material for building solid paragraphs that, in turn, become the well-written article. On the other hand, poorly written sentences doom the article to failure at the outset. To construct well-written sentences, you should avoid weak expletives, flabby prose, overly long sentences and awkward syntax and stilted language.

Weak Expletives

Starting a sentence with the weak expletive *There is* or *There are* wastes reading time and puts the reader on hold until the sentence topic finally appears. Why risk losing a reader because of the weak expletive when this impediment is unnecessary and can be easily eliminated?

Consider the following sentences:

There is nothing that the mayor likes better than to spend the day fishing at the lake.

There are many people who will benefit from the new tax laws.

There were many women in history who could have been capable leaders had society allowed them the opportunity.

There is a lot of pressure placed on college students to drink at fraternity parties.

There are quite a few extracurricular activities available to students on the Montcalm State University campus.

There were many people at the demonstration in front of the student union building.

Each sentence may contain important information for a hard news or feature article, but the reader has to wait until the third or fourth word, or even later, to learn the subject of the sentence. To learn what has happened, the reader must read even more words. To avoid such delays, restructure the sentences and place the subject as near to the beginning of the sentence as you can.

The mayor likes nothing better than to spend the day fishing at the lake.

Many people will benefit from the new tax laws.

Many women in history could have been capable leaders had society allowed them the opportunity.

College students at fraternity parties face a lot of pressure to drink.

More than 50 extracurricular activities are available to students on the Montcalm State University campus.

Many people were at the demonstration in front of the student union building.

Reread both versions of each sentence. Observe how much stronger the revised sentences are than the original sentences that begin with the weak expletives. The revised sentences are alive and interesting, providing the reader with actors, actions and direction. These sentences reach the point quickly. Such writing encourages readers to continue reading an article, and that is your goal as a writer.

Flabby Prose

Flabby prose is filled with needless words and phrases that obscure the point of your writing. Look at the following sentences and see how many words you can strike and still retain the basic information of the sentence.

It is a fact that few students in Longwood High School would like to see the school year lengthened.

We are pretty unhappy with the reason for which you have decided not to accept our offer.

The student government president stated that he was a little shocked by the tendency of a large number of his constituents to criticize him in public.

The parking problem, for the most part, is one that will have to be dealt with by a special committee that has been created for the purpose of considering the problem.

These sentences drag and make the reader trudge through needless words and phrases. Cut out the unnecessary words and listen to the resulting improved rhythm and flow of the sentences.

> Few students in Longwood High School would like to see the school year lengthened.

(Omit "It is a fact" and simply state the fact.)

> We are unhappy with your decision to refuse our offer.

(*Pretty* is a worthless modifier because it is vague. The decision to refuse the offer, not "The reason for which you have decided," is what makes the writer unhappy.)

> The student government president stated that he was shocked by the public criticism of many constituents.

(How much is a "little shocked"? Avoid the vague use of *little*. Why not use fewer words to express the already vague "a large number"? Do you believe that the "tendency" to criticize instead of the actual criticism shocks the president?)

> A special committee will deal with the parking problem.

(What function does "for the most part" serve? Whether the problem is one of many or the only one, what benefit is gained by describing it as "one that will have to be dealt with"? Is a "special committee" indication enough to readers that the committee is dedicated to the problem, or must the writer add "that has been created for the purpose of considering the problem"? Why use the passive voice, placing the subject last?)

Sharpen your writing by avoiding empty words and needless phrases. Even if you are being paid by the word, resist the urge to "pad" the writing. The point of writing is to be published, a goal you will fail to reach with flabby, padded writing.

Overly Long Sentences

Overly long sentences present a different problem from sentences infected by flabby prose. Writers produce overly long sentences when they attempt to string together too many important ideas between a pair of periods. Writers sometimes fall into this error because they are afraid of writing "choppy" prose. Choppy prose is the result of a continuous stream of very brief sentences, each stating a key idea, with no connecting terms to link the sentences. Some hard news topics require such prose, but most writing, especially feature articles, benefit from the coordination of ideas. How can a writer decide when to pare all but the basic idea from a sentence? Intuition plays a big role, but attention to the subject and to your angle on that subject plays an even bigger role in the choice.

The sin of the overly long sentence is most obvious in the lead paragraph. You should limit the lead sentence, even the *summary* lead sentence, to 35 words or fewer. The following sentence may include substantial information, but such information is worthless if too many words make its meaning unclear to the reader.

> According to a release provided to the press by the office of the mayor and containing information that was gathered through several surveys with residents of the city as well as research into state and county legislative records with further information provided by the federal government and including data obtained and analyzed in a period covering the past two years, the city council has decided to consider some means of obtaining funding to aid in the repairs of homes owned by a specific group of residents of the city who are in need of assistance.

The preceding one-sentence paragraph is unclear, despite the writer's contention that all of the included information is vital to understanding the issue. Of course, a sentence containing 95 words is unusual. Readers of both hard news and feature articles would never see it, because a copy editor would trim it to a manageable length long before the final copy is typeset. Despite its lack of value in an article, this example is still valuable here. It shows a lack of restraint: Writers often become carried away with their descriptions, and beginning writers are not as economical in their word use as those who are experienced.

If this were your sentence, how would you trim it before your article reached the copy editor? What is the *point* of the sentence? What is necessary and what is unnecessary? Keep the necessary information and reserve the rest for possible use later in the article.

What does the sentence announce? Must the reader know the sources of the data reviewed in preparation for the mayor's press release? Must the reader know the time frame in which the data were gathered?

Before providing readers with an extensive background for a political announcement, provide them with the announcement:

> The city council hopes to obtain funding to help needy residents repair their homes.

Everything else that appears in the original 95-word sentence can be developed into supporting ideas following the lead. If you examine the original carefully, you will find that some of the information is redundant and can be eliminated.

Awkward Syntax and Stilted Language

The two faults of awkward syntax and stilted language are not identical, but both require that writers fine-tune their ears to *hear* these errors in their writing. Awkward syntax occurs in sentences that contain variations of the familiar word order of subject-verb-object. Stilted language occurs in pompously written sentences that use words and word orders meant to impress rather than to communicate.

Awkward sentences are often the result of fast writing and sloppy editing. When writers read their sentences aloud, they often hear the awkwardness and find ways to correct it. Look at the following sentence that one writer left in the draft of an article given to a newspaper copy editor:

That he had no family on whom to depend was a concern of his.

The sentence does not flow smoothly because of the word order. A better version expresses the same idea and uses many of the same words, but they are placed into a more familiar pattern:

His concern was that he had no family to depend on.

The order is the familiar subject-verb-object form that flows more smoothly for most readers.

The *stilted language* error is the result of a pretentious tone and ostentatious language that causes a stilted structure. Some editors describe stilted language as the type of language used by academics making a speech at a conference, or the language of an orator whose goal is to impress an audience. Some writers might describe stilted language as mere snobbishness. Whichever definition you prefer, the harm in stilted language is that it turns readers off. Stilted language appears to be condescending, and readers do not like condescension.

How do you correct this error? Read possibly offensive sentences aloud and let your ear judge. Then rewrite the offenders to sound as if you were speaking to a friend or neighbor without the desire to dazzle and impress. Consider how to improve the following sentence:

They were devastated by the board of education's recently instituted draconian regulations, the pedagogues whose task it is to impart knowledge to the offspring of this worthy microcosm of society.

Draconian? Pedagogues? Worthy microcosm of society? Many readers would be put off by the pretentious language, even if they were familiar with the words. If this sentence appeared in an article about new restrictions placed on teachers in a given city, which is the topic, most readers would simply move on and ignore this sentence and the rest of the article. This show of erudition might be satisfying to the writer, but what value does it have if no one reads the rest of the article? The following sentence expresses the same concern phrased in language that interests rather than repels readers:

Teachers in this multicultural city are upset by the board of education's strict new policies.

What more is needed to express the concern? The pretentious language and tone of the original sentence lends nothing to its meaning or importance.

ORGANIZING PARAGRAPHS

After the sentence, the paragraph is the next important building block in writing the article. The key to successful paragraph construction in hard news and feature article writing is to ignore certain guidelines you learned in elementary and high school grammar classes. You were cautioned that the well-made paragraph for essays begins with a topic sentence, followed by several support sentences and ending with a concluding or "clincher" sentence. This is not the format for the paragraphs in magazine articles, and paragraphing in newspapers deviates even more drastically.

Most hard news articles contain brief paragraphs of two or three sentences, none of them a topic sentence. Instead, each paragraph represents one point in the overall body of information presented in the newspaper article. Paragraphs are tools for making the information manageable, each starting when a new idea begins, but not actually flowing smoothly from the preceding idea. Hard news article paragraphs are actually like a child's building blocks, all part of a larger common entity but without a visible connective thread to bind them.

Each paragraph is a somewhat independent unit of thought. A paragraph may be moved around or incorporated into other paragraphs or subsections of an article, placed wherever it affords the greatest use in explaining the subject.

To decide the way to organize the paragraphs in your article, begin by listing all of the points that you want to discuss. The list works like an outline, but you do not need to establish major and minor headings or subheadings. Review the list to rule out any ideas that do not deal directly with the topic; then develop each of the listed items into one or more paragraphs. The same point, developed in a paragraph, might be used in different areas of an article. When one of those paragraphs appears to contain several points, and if you can write two or three sentences about each point, then form new paragraphs.

Several clear guidelines exist for starting new paragraphs:

- Begin a new paragraph whenever you include quotations and a new speaker begins.
- Begin a new paragraph for each new quotation if you alternate speakers.
- Begin a new paragraph when your focus changes from one person to another, from one locale to another, or from one time to another.
- Begin a new paragraph when you discuss the other side of the story or someone's opposing view on an issue.

The pauses that you create with these breaks allow readers time to switch emphasis of thought. This change in emphasis places increased importance on the writing that follows the break, writing that might have been ignored or de-emphasized if it were included at the end of the previous paragraph. Review the way the independent units function in the following example:

> Few people met the legendary poet Allen Ginsberg and walked away unchanged by the experience. He was a man who impressed others by his mere presence.
>
> "I only met him once," states one middle-aged woman, "but his kindness and wisdom are forever in my memory."
>
> "He was a radical hippie who rocked society, and then was rewarded by the very society he sneered at," notes a former Brooklyn College student of his.
>
> Raised in Paterson, New Jersey, in a culturally and politically mixed environment, Allen Ginsberg sought to relate to all people. His political views were radically liberal, yet he was an advocate for peace, not violent revolution. He embraced Buddhism, yet retained much of his Jewish heritage.

> Newspapers of the 1960s recorded his opposition to the war in Vietnam. Photographs showed him slipping the stems of daffodils into the rifle barrels of National Guardsmen sent to disperse demonstrators. He often spoke out against the war at public gatherings, and his poems contained antiwar fervor.
>
> Ginsberg became a target of the FBI because of his political activities. Then-Director J. Edgar Hoover ordered agents to gather information about the poet's activities. The eventual file ran to several thousand pages.

The paragraphs in the preceding selection from a feature article written soon after the death of Beat poet Allen Ginsberg are individual packets of information. They are connected by their central topic, but their structure does not follow the grammarian's approach to the well-made paragraph. None of the paragraphs contains a rigidly structured topic sentence with the requisite support and clincher sentences. Despite this, the article does convey a unity that is evident in the rest of the article.

EXPLOITING THE POTENTIAL OF GRAMMAR

Grammar counts. Do not make a copy editor take responsibility for second-guessing your meaning in a sentence. Carefully read and revise your work to eliminate the all-too-common errors that continue to appear in print.

Misplaced modifiers, subject-verb disagreement and pronoun-antecedent disagreement wreak havoc with sentence meaning. Punctuation, even one misplaced comma, can make your writing express ideas that are alien to your intention. Ambiguity, inaccuracy and obscured meaning are the results of careless grammar. Why risk having such charges leveled at your writing? Grammar errors can be controlled.

Misplaced Modifiers

Review the following sentences and determine the writer's meaning in each. Observe the effect of the bold words on the rest of the sentence.

> **At the age of three,** the author's mother died and left him orphaned.
>
> The student demonstrators who chanted and carried signs made their point effectively **in front of the student union building.**
>
> The police chief **on the seven o'clock news** responded honestly to reporters' questions about the robbery.
>
> **By wearing a dress, high-heeled shoes and a wig,** the FBI representative reported that the spy had escaped detection.

Each of the preceding sentences contains a misplaced modifier error that creates humor in some instances and inaccurate expression in all instances. Is it logical that the author's mother had a child before the age of three? In the second sentence, is *where* the point was effectively made the issue, as the sentence indicates? Does the writer of the third sentence seek to emphasize that the police chief (any police chief) on the given news program responded honestly, or is the issue a specific police chief who responded honestly in a given venue? In the fourth sentence, is the FBI agent wearing the elaborate disguise?

The meaning is sometimes obvious despite the misplaced modifier, as in the first sentence, but the remaining sentences pose a problem. A copy editor would have to waste time by contacting the writer to determine actual meaning in the sentence before repositioning the modifier. Consider how the meaning in each sentence changes when the modifier is correctly placed.

> **When the author was three,** his mother died and left him orphaned.
>
> The student demonstrators who chanted and carried **signs in front of the student union building** made their point effectively.
>
> **On the seven o'clock news,** the police chief responded honestly to reporters' questions about the robbery.
>
> The FBI representative reported that the spy had escaped detection **by wearing a dress, high-heeled shoes and a wig.**

Subject-Verb Agreement

Students learn early in their experiences with grammar that the subject of a sentence must always agree with the verb. A singular subject requires a singular verb. A plural subject requires a plural verb. The rules seem simple, but errors in subject-verb agreement continue to appear in newspaper and magazine articles. Many such errors occur in sentences that contain indefinite pronouns, intervening phrases, clauses between the subject and the verb, or the compound subject using *or*. Most of these errors are preventable when writers know the rules.

Review the following sentences and identify the reason for the error in each:

Each of the church elders give a weekly donation to the cause of the missions on other continents.

Either the council members or the mayor are expected at the rally.

None of the choir members want to go to the South Westfield competition.

The teacher or the students is held responsible for any damage to the building.

The board of education ruled that a teacher on academic leave and receiving half-salary need verification of her status.

Two of the errors in the preceding sentences occur because the writers are unclear regarding the rules governing subjects other than nouns. Two additional errors result from the confusion of agreement when *or* is used in the subject. The final error results from the distance between the subject and the verb that the intervening phrase creates.

Each of the church elders **gives** a weekly donation to the cause of the missions on other continents.

(The subject is *each,* an indefinite pronoun that always takes a singular verb.)

Either the council members or the mayor is expected at the rally.

(When a compound subject using *or* appears in a sentence, the part of the subject nearest the verb determines the number of the verb. In this case, *mayor* is singular, so the verb must be singular.)

None of the choir members **wants** to go to the South Westfield competition.

(The subject is *none,* an indefinite pronoun that usually takes a singular verb.)

The teacher or the students **are** held responsible for any damage to the building.

(When a compound subject using *or* appears in a sentence, the part of the subject nearest the verb determines the number of the verb. In this case, *students* is plural, so the verb must be plural.)

The board of education ruled that a teacher on academic leave and receiving half-salary **needs** verification of her status.

(The subject *teacher* is singular, so the verb must be singular, despite the intervening words.)

To avoid these errors, remember several rules:

- Indefinite pronouns are those such as *no one, everyone, everybody, somebody* and others that do not refer to a specific person or thing. These pronouns *always* take the singular form of the verb.
- When *or* is used to form a compound subject, the number of the noun nearest the verb determines the number of the verb. Thus, "James or the band members" requires a plural verb, but "the band members or James" requires a singular verb.

Pronoun Reference Errors

Pronouns should agree in number with their antecedents (the nouns to which they refer). References in a sentence must be clear, and readers should not be required to sort out the pronouns and match them to the correct antecedents. That job should be completed by the writer before publication. Why, then, do sentences similar to the following continue to appear in print?

> Too many people idolize rock stars, and they give little credence to stories about their drug use or to their personal lives.
> Everybody in this city knows their way to the fairgrounds.
> A woman in medical school 50 years ago had to expect many nasty comments to be made by male students against them.
> The mayor or the council members will be held responsible for his decision to close the school.
> If a student does not have good study skills, he will have difficulty succeeding in college.

The preceding sentences, which illustrate three types of pronoun reference errors, are taken from published hard news or feature articles. The first example creates pronoun confusion and forces the reader to struggle to understand the writer's references. The errors in the second and fourth sentences occur because the writer has forgotten the rules governing indefinite pronouns and those regarding the compound subject containing *or*. In the third sentence, the distance created by the words that intervene between the pronoun and its antecedent makes the writer careless.

The error in the final sentence occurs more frequently today because of the increased emphasis on political correctness. In the past, non-sex-specific nouns such as *student, teacher, reader* and others routinely received the male pronoun reference *he*. Sensitivity to the sexism implied in this automatic reference has led writers to use such awkward references as *he or she, she or he, he/she, s/he* or the plural non-sex-specific *they*. The last choice creates a grammar error.

Is there a solution? Of course, and it is a solution that most recently published grammar and journalism handbooks recommend. Use the plural form of the non-sex-specific noun; then use the plural pronoun references *they* or *them*.

> Too many people idolize rock stars and give little credence to stories about their drug use or their personal lives.
> People in this city know their way to the fairgrounds.

A woman in medical school 50 years ago had to expect many nasty comments against her to be made by male students.

The mayor or the council members will be held responsible for their decision to close the school.

Students who do not have good study skills will have difficulty succeeding in college.

Punctuation

Some punctuation errors in newspaper and magazine articles are minor, leading at most to embarrassment for the writer and humor for the reader. Other errors can have serious consequences. This section highlights the most common errors.

Periods. A period usually ends a declarative or imperative sentence, but confusion occurs when quotation marks and parentheses are used with the period. The period is always placed inside the quotation marks, but parentheses require more thought. If a complete sentence is placed within parentheses, the period is also placed within them. If the parentheses hold only a phrase, the period appears outside.

Several recent graduates of the local high school expect to enlist in the United States Marine Corps, each hoping to become "one of a few good men."

The high rate of recidivism among young drug addicts has alarming consequences for everyone in this nation. (See the related profile elsewhere in this issue.)

The new clean air standards (still to be voted on by the legislature) will decrease the number of respiratory ailments suffered by children.

Question marks and exclamation points. These end punctuation marks are not placed within quotation marks unless an entire sentence ending in one of these forms of punctuation is quoted. When you are quoting an individual who has asked a question, the usual comma after the quotation and before the attribution is replaced by the question mark. The same rules apply when quoting exclamations.

Have you read "The Rime of the Ancient Mariner"?

The reporter asked, "What is the benefit to this new health plan?"
"What can we do while we wait for the police?" the manager asked.
"Nothing will ever be the same!" the woman screamed.

Commas. Writers often find that commas are a source of confusion, especially because news style differs from grammar handbooks in some uses.

When quotation marks are used, place the commas within the quotation marks.

Separate items in a series by commas, but omit the comma before the conjunction *unless* doing so creates confusion.

Use commas after the exact date and year when both are given, but omit commas if only the month and the year are printed.

Use commas to set off appositives (words or phrases that rename a noun) and nonrestrictive (unnecessary) phrases.

Do not use commas between closely related words in a name.

The young marine had hoped to become "one of a few good men," but he succeeded in learning only what he did not like about military service.

The local union held a fund-raising breakfast that offered participants a choice of coffee, tea, juice, pastries, muffins, pancakes, and bacon and eggs.

Few people in this town will ever forget that December 7, 1941, was the beginning of a new era.

The tornado ripped through the center of town in May 1996 and caught us offguard.

James Hilton, the last mayor of the decade, left office on a note of prosperity.

Political observers predict that George Bush Jr. will run for the office of President of the United States.

Semicolons. This punctuation mark is used to eliminate comma confusion by separating items in a series if those items contain commas. Unlike standard rules of grammar, newspaper style requires that the semicolon be used before the conjunction as well. Only rarely do newspapers omit the coordinating conjunction and employ the semi-colon to link independent clauses.

> Local delegates to the convention include the mayor, James Stevens; the court clerk, Rita Allworth; and the school superintendent, John DeNyl.

Dash and colon. Each of these forms of punctuation has a different use, but writers frequently confuse their functions. Use the dash sparingly and mainly for effect. Set off terms within a sentence or to make a dramatic point at the end by using the dash. Use the colon at the end of a sentence to introduce a list, a specific explanatory sentence after the main sentence, or an explanatory list.

> Many people who knew the diva—both admirers and detractors—appeared at her funeral.
> The candidates will debate tomorrow evening—if the expected tidal wave does not hit our beachfront community.
> After attending classes, a student has only three needs: food, a bed and cable television.

By now, you are aware that no detail is small enough to overlook in your writing. Readers may be very forgiving, and you may have such dazzling ideas that others will overlook even glaring errors of presentation. These possibilities are irrelevant to the good writer. Writing articles for newspapers and magazines requires not only talent and skill, but also a dedication to putting forth your best effort, even in regard to the smallest of details.

Chapter Five

Creating Invisible Transitions

The well-written hard news or feature article should contain transitions that are effective in moving readers from one point to the next. Good transitions require the writer to have the sleight of hand of a good magician, maintaining the logical flow of ideas in the article without becoming heavy-handed.

The reader needs to feel that a logical link exists between the points of discussion in an article. And the job of the writer is to show how it all fits together without interrupting the flow of the writing. The crutches that you were taught to use in writing essays in the English classroom are useful at only some points in the article narrative. Most effective transitions in articles written for newspapers and magazines are not so obvious as such well-worn phrases as "for the most part," "on the other hand," and "seen from a different viewpoint."

In the well-organized story, material in one paragraph should create the need for a follow-up in the next paragraph. Raise questions that readers might ask, and then give answers in paragraphs that follow. Offer observations and generalizations that provoke a desire in readers for more information, and then provide that information. If a story has been so well structured that every effect is foreshadowed by a cause, every answer is foreshadowed by a question, and every fact or quotation is foreshadowed by a intriguing generalization, the writer will not have to fall back on obvious crutches.

THE BUILDING BLOCK APPROACH

Recall the guidelines for starting paragraphs in Chapter Four. The method of transition is one that would not hold up in a grammar handbook. News style, however, uses the building block approach to report much hard news.

Begin by listing all of the points that are relevant for discussion in your article, and sort out the points of emphasis. Consider the continuing story of the student demonstration at the fictional Montcalm State University, a story used for illustrating several techniques in earlier chapters. Ignoring order for now, list every point that can be made in a hard news article about the demonstration.

1. Composition of the group demonstrating
2. Reason for the demonstration
3. Means of demonstration
4. Site and its importance
5. Goals of the demonstrators
6. Nondemonstrators in attendance
7. Reactions of nondemonstrators
8. Immediate results

A hard news article provides readers with the facts regarding an occurrence, and the preceding list promises a logical discussion of just the facts. You might choose to combine points one and two into a strong lead statement, and perhaps to move one or two other points into different positions. The resulting article should lead readers to anticipate the next point. They will if you cluster descriptions of the demonstrators and nondemonstrators together, the activities with the choice of site, and the reactions with the goals, and then end with the expected results.

If the demonstration occurs over more than a few hours, you might change the organizing principles of the list to create a chronological list of occurrences. You would then weave the other items from the list into the chronological narrative.

Your goal as the writer is to help readers understand the topic. Moving from the simplest concept in the list (the people) to the most complex (the results) allows you and your readers to build on the information that has come before. In this approach, no quantum mental leaps occur.

THE JIGSAW PUZZLE APPROACH

The key to successful and subtle transitions is consistency among the points discussed in the article. The list created and organized to report news of the demonstration becomes virtually useless if you plan to write an article that profiles the students. An article based on this focus requires another list—one developed from the first point.

Listing points for a profile of the student demonstrators illustrates a second means of transition: the jigsaw puzzle approach. How do you want to approach the topic? Will your article be an overview? Or will you focus on individual demonstrators? Will physical description be sufficient? Or will you elicit information regarding their personal lives? Are their majors important to the discussion? Will you identify their individual goals?

All of these points combine to provide a comprehensive view of the demonstrators. Using the jigsaw puzzle method of providing transition, *how* you organize the points is less important than whether you provide *linkages* within paragraphs. Such linkages are words or phrases that create a bridge from one paragraph to the next.

Repetition of a key word in the preceding paragraph is one effective way of transporting the reader from one paragraph to another. To work, however, the repeated word must be a noun, a vivid adjective or adverb, or a strong verb. Consider the following paragraphs:

Student demonstrators who gathered last week at Montcalm State University were a diverse group, but they shared a **common** goal. They united to protest the recent state-mandated tuition increase, a concern that overshadowed race, sex, age and geographic concerns.

> Some locked arms and chanted while others permeated the group with slogan-covered signs, but all had found a common enemy . . .

The opening paragraph presents many possibilities, but the focus of the article about the demonstration is on the way in which students united against one cause, a *common* cause. Because of this theme, *common* is the most effective word to repeat so that the writer can create a transition to the first sentence of the second paragraph. This choice does not prevent the writer from selecting one of the differences suggested in the first paragraph and developing it fully. The function of this linkage is to connect immediately the first and second paragraphs for readers, before they sense any gaps in the flow of ideas.

Another linkage is the use of parallelism in constructing sentences, a technique in which rhythm and sound reinforce meaning. The transition occurs because readers "hear" in their minds a similarity that creates coherence of thought. Of course, a writer cannot depend on sound alone to maintain a transition if the topic changes radically from one paragraph to the next. Read the following sentences aloud and listen to the way in which the sound of their parallel structures provides a bridge between paragraphs.

> The first-year students feared that no seniors would join them, but ten demonstrated. The undergraduates did not expect to see graduates, but twenty appeared. The day provided several good surprises.
>
> The scholarship students expected that only they had an interest, but other students joined them. The part-time students worried that they would not be taken seriously, but they were welcomed. The day brought people closer.

Parallelism in sentence construction is difficult to maintain throughout a long article, but it is very effective in quickly making your point in a short article. Even if you could continue the same constructions through numerous paragraphs, the result would soon become repetitive. This linkage is best used sparingly.

THE CHRONOLOGICAL APPROACH

Most writers are familiar with chronology and time references that give a time order to events and actions. The most obvious and overused linkage of this sort begins each paragraph with a different time term:

> **First,** the students decided on a strategy. . .
> **Second,** demonstrators drew attention to. . .
> **Third,** those in the line. . . .
> Finally, those remaining. . .

As you have already learned, this approach is only one step above simply numbering the ideas and offering readers a list. It is unimaginative and quickly bores readers. Creating an article of any significant length is also difficult. Once begun, the counting has to continue. How many paragraphs would you read before throwing the newspaper or magazine aside in annoyance?

Another way of approaching the time reference transition is to begin paragraphs with words such as *before, after, now, later, since, three days afterward* and so on. Instead of simply providing a numbered list, the writer who uses these terms sets events in context and in relation to each other.

If your article follows the development of an incident or covers a person's life over several days, weeks, months or years, then use these units of time to provide transition. The days of the week or months of the year provide handy guideposts for establishing chronology as well as allowing the reader to anticipate each paragraph.

The successful writer uses these techniques to subtly show readers the time sequence—without having to tell them that the article has moved on. The smoothly flowing article does not use such terms as signposts to begin paragraphs. Instead, the terms appear through the writing, moving readers along at the beginning, middle and end.

Using a combination of the numbering terms and the context transition words, you can effectively take your readers from the beginning through the end of an incident or a life without creating breaks in the word flow. Less frequently, all three chronological transition techniques are combined. In either case, the emphasis is on subtlety in their application.

Examine how the chronological transitions function in the following example. Note that the writer weaves the terms throughout the narrative, instead of simply using them to separate chunks of information.

The strike has consumed the lives of people in this small town, most of whom work for the Fastcar Gear Company. No one **five decades ago** could have known that the company they had reluctantly accepted would **today** be its only hope for survival. How could such a revolution in the economy occur?

The town had tasted prosperity in the years **before** World War II. Small, family-owned textile mills had flourished, and the main drag of town was cluttered with stores. Some blame the war for the change. **After** returning home from military service, many men no longer wanted to work in the mills. Several of the mills had closed **during** the war, leaving few jobs for those who were still interested. The mood was right **in 1947** when the Fastcar Gear Company proposed building a plant . . .

The move toward a strike occurred gradually, as the **second** step in a carefully prepared union plan. Talks scheduled for **June** ended in a stalemate, leaving both union and management to sweat through the **summer.** Both looked with concern toward **September,** when the current contract would end.

The article is concerned with the present strike by workers at the Fastcar Gear Company, but the writer knows that readers need a background to the problem. The explanations of why this industry is so important and how long that importance has dominated the town provide a foundation for establishing the serious nature of the strike.

The writer must also explain two chronologies: how the company gained a dominant role in the economy of the town and how the strike evolved. The chronological transitions might have appeared at the beginnings of sentences, but structuring the article in that manner would result in monotony.

THE SPATIAL APPROACH

The writer who uses the spatial approach attempts to give the article a physical context within which to explore the topic. Transitions of this sort can name specific places and identify specific distances, or such transitions may provide generalizations and vague indications of direction. Both types of spatial transitions usually appear in prepositional phrases, forming adverb modifiers that tell readers *where.*

> Allison left home after high school to pursue a career as a writer **in New York** . . .
>
> . . . She had trouble writing during the day because her cramped apartment, located **in the worst neighborhood in the city,** shook constantly with the sounds of the rumbling "L" and the slamming of nearby doors.
>
> . . . the withered old man lying in the street. As she further surveyed the crowded streets that formed her new home, she saw less to please her. Down the block. . .

The preceding article is a profile of the early years of a now successful writer. Because the focus is on the use of spatial transitions, the colorful descriptions are largely omitted. (For more on the use of descriptions, see Chapter Seven.) Observe the way in which the reader is brought into New York City in the opening. Then transitions are used to narrow the physical area to the neighborhood, the street and the block.

The preceding example is only one of many ways in which the writer might have conveyed the sense of place to readers. The distance in feet or meters from the subject's front door to the old man might have given more immediacy to the observation. Instead of merely characterizing Allison's new surroundings as "the worst neighborhood in the city," the writer might have named it and the streets surrounding. Somewhere in the article, the writer must also name Allison's hometown, as well as the stores in which she shops and where she goes in the new environment.

Although the subject of the article is the individual and not the environment, Allison's surroundings can offer an important look at her early influences. Her introduction to the city, with all of the attendant adventures, creates a physical context that can be influential.

One note of caution is necessary about the use of spatial transitions. They are valuable only if the physical context is really a part of the narrative. In this example, the writer achieves that goal, but such relevance cannot be forced and expected to result in a cohesive narrative.

A different angle on the subject would require different types of transitions. If the focus of the article were Allison's techniques of writing, the reader would need to know little more than where she sits when writing. With this focus in an article, the spatial transitions become useless.

THE QUOTATION APPROACH

Quotations are valuable resources that perform various functions in an article. (For more on the use of quotations, see Chapter Eight.) Only one function of quotations—their value as transitions—is of interest in this chapter.

Quotations that end paragraphs provide a natural lead-in to the next paragraph. Only quotations that express views are of value in an article, so a response must follow. The writer may explain the quotation, discuss its significance, link it to the situation under discussion or refute its importance.

A good transition quotation should evoke a response that advances the writer's purpose in an article. That is why you have to choose quotations carefully and discard those that are weak, rambling, noncommittal or vaguely impersonal. Readers' eyes usually gravitate to quotations, so disperse transition quotations throughout your article, to keep the reader moving to the end.

Consider how different the following example would be without the quotation transitions to maintain the narrative flow:

Who are the newest millionaires in America today? Are they the Wall Street whiz kids made rich on one smart stock transaction? The Silicon Valley geniuses whose technological know-how has transformed the nation? Neither.

"I didn't know what I was signing fifteen years ago," states shop foreman James. "I needed a job, so I signed every line marked with an 'X'."

You might call James an accidental millionaire. One of the lines that he signed asked if he wanted to have a steady five percent taken from his pay. With wage increases and growing interest rates, that five percent has made him a millionaire. And he still has fifteen years until retirement.

He is one member of a growing club, people whose 401k plans guarantee them a comfortable retirement.

"If I don't have it, I don't spend it," asserts Gina, an assembly worker in a packaging plant and soon to be a millionaire herself. "Oh, I've sometimes wished that those extra dollars could have been kicking around in my pocket, but 18 years later I'd rather have the money saved. Who knows what I would have spent it on?"

The ease with which their money has accumulated surprises most of the new millionaires. . .

The article can take any of several directions, depending on the word count required and the writer's purpose. In this article, quotations from two of the "newest millionaires" appear and exhibit a similar theme. Both have accumulated their wealth through savings plans at work, so readers have a good indication that the article will probably focus on this method to financial security. The article will probably take a positive approach to the subject, because both quotations are positive in tone. A further indication of the direction of the article is the identification of both speakers as blue-collar workers.

The writer uses both quotations to provide transitions between the points discussed. The first quotation creates interest with its teasing content, leaving readers to read further to learn what James actually signed away. The quotation sets the stage for the writer to explain in a paragraph that demystifies the statements. This explanatory paragraph is anticipated by readers after they read the first quotation. The paragraph also begins to reveal the topic of the article.

The second quotation promotes another point that the writer wants to discuss in the article, the ease of using 401k plans to accumulate wealth. Letting Gina express her initial hesitance to having money taken from her pay, and then her recognition that she would have misspent it, anticipates another paragraph of explanation. The writer will now examine the impact of the plans on a person's day-to-day life and the rewards that will accrue.

Additional quotations should maintain the tone of approval toward the topic, although the experienced writer can include even negative comments and use them as transitions. The trick is in choosing the right quotation, one that provides a contrast to the main theme of the article but which is not so convincing that the quotation negates all that has been said.

The best transitions are those that your reader never sees. The beginning writer often has difficulty in making the relatively seamless connections between ideas that the approaches discussed here provide. Such skill comes with continued experience in writing—putting words, sentences and paragraphs together to create articles. As you increase in your skill, you will find yourself less likely to rely on the crutches, those handy words and phrases that serve as the glue between your thoughts.

Chapter Six

Choosing the Right Word(s)

How can you make your writing reach out and grab a reader's attention? Clear, concise and consistent writing requires strong verbs, precise diction, active rather than passive voice, and bias-free language.

VIBRANT VERBS

Nothing is more dull than a hard news or feature article filled with weak verbs. Some writers become accustomed to using a small group of "safe" verbs from which they rarely deviate, leaving readers only to imagine the range of actions attached to the subject of the article. Other writers fall into the "got" trap, substituting a form of "to get" in the place of many other verbs having precise meanings, leaving copy editors to become creative with their substitutions. Either way, the writer who shuns vibrant verbs ignores an important means of exciting reader interest and actually cheats readers of information.

Verb Variety
Language is rich with possibilities, so why settle for boring verbs? Consider how much more interesting you can make the following sentences by substituting strong action verbs for the bland choices of the writer.

Example:

The mayor **walked** out of the council meeting after Dr. Orson **suggested** changes in the housing authority code.

Do the words that appear in boldface create a strong visual image? Did the mayor overreact when he *walked* out of a meeting after someone merely *suggested* changes? If this is the story, then keep the verbs as they are. If, however, the mayor was angered, he might have *stormed, stomped, rushed* or *barreled* out of the meeting. And to what is he reacting? Might Dr. Orson have done more than *suggested* changes? What if he *demanded, ordered, required* or *advocated* these changes? Would readers then attach more importance to the actions of both men? To the implications of these actions? Would you be tempted to read further to learn more about the issue? Of course, most readers would be drawn into the situation because conflict is always interesting.

Now look at the following sentence and see how changing the verbs can make the writing come alive. Also observe the way in which *meaning* changes when substitutions are made.

Example 1:

The caretaker **took** the gold statue and **placed** it into the closet.

Example 2:

The caretaker **stole** the gold statue and **hid** it in the closet.

Example 3:

The caretaker **removed** the gold statue and **stored** it in the closet.

Example 4:

The caretaker **confiscated** the gold statue and **safeguarded** it in the closet.

By changing one or both verbs, the writer effectively changes readers' perceptions of the caretaker. Is he simply carrying out an expected task, as Examples 1 and 3 imply? Is he a thief, as Example 2 suggests? Or has he recognized the statue as illegally obtained property and put it aside until proper authorities can take possession of it? The choice of verbs makes the difference in the writer's message and the readers' understanding of the story by adding more specific meaning to the action.

The "Get" Glut

Dealing with the "get" glut calls upon your skills in achieving both verb variety and precise diction. Many lazy writers of hard news and feature articles overuse forms of the verb *to get*. They strain the time and the talents of copy editors who must find substitutions that add variety and specific action to the writing.

How can you avoid this pitfall? The most effective means of avoiding the "get" glut is to remain alert to your overuse of that verb. Become adept at using more specific verbs to accurately say what you mean.

Look at the use of to get in the following sentences. How can each be more effective? What verb can you substitute in each to make the action more specific?

Example 1:

How much money do you **get** each week as a teacher?

Example 2:

I don't **get** what you mean by that response.

Example 3:

The school district is hoping to **get** $3 million in federal funds.

Example 4:

The scholarship winner was able to **get** high grades throughout her high school career.

Example 5:

We were not able to **get** a quote from the mayor.

What is missing in these sentences? All five sentences resort to using the weak, nonexpressive verb *get*, instead of exploiting the potential of strong action verbs. Observe how much more expressive each question or statement becomes when a strong verb is substituted.

Example 1:

How much money do you **earn** each week as a teacher?

Example 2:

I don't **understand** what you mean by that response.

Example 3:

The school district is hoping to **receive** $3 million in federal funds.

Example 4:

The scholarship winner was able to **achieve** high grades throughout her high school career.

Example 5:

We were not able to **elicit** a quote from the mayor.

These are only five of many specific verbs that should be used to replace forms of get in all writing.

PRECISE DICTION

The hard news article demands that the writer provide precise information and use precise diction to convey the most accurate and detailed information available. The soft news or feature article may not be concerned with breaking news, but the feature writer is no less responsible for providing readers with the same accuracy and precision in detail. Unlike the focus on using specific and precise verbs in previous sections, the concern with precise diction covers all of the language in your articles.

Why is precise diction important? Writing is communication. The article that uses vague or imprecise nouns, verbs or modifiers communicates only generalizations to readers who are then left to their own devices in interpreting your meaning. Imprecise language just implies action or information, and it leaves readers to infer what they will. Can you be certain that readers will accurately infer what you intend to communicate in your writing?

Why do readers need to know that "50 people were killed in the crash" rather than "a number of people were killed in the crash"?

Must you specify that "the fireworks burst into colorful red, blue and orange shooting stars" instead of "the fireworks burst into multicolored stars"?

Will readers be more interested in knowing that "the campus police stopped a car that was speeding through campus at 70 miles per hour" rather than "the campus police stopped a car that was speeding through campus"?

Are you accurate to report that "a fire destroyed stores in the strip mall" if the stores are damaged but they will not have to be rebuilt?

If only six out of 45 student government representatives voted in favor of a campus curfew, are you playing fair with readers to write that "a number of" or "some" of them did?

Adverbs and adjectives must also be judiciously chosen and used only if they provide needed information in an article. Vague, generalized modifiers just provide word clutter in a sentence. If overused, they can detract from the main points of the material.

Many writers feel that they must provide adverbs to describe every quotation of speakers cited in their articles. Thus, writers adorn simple statements with such emotion-laden adverbs as *mournfully, hopefully, sarcastically, sadly* and other terms that are often more a reflection of the writer's perceptions than an accurate representation of the speaker's feelings. Allow the words of the people whom you quote in your articles to stand alone. If you have chosen the quotations wisely, they will reveal the appropriate emotions to readers.

Adjectives also pose problems for many writers of articles, many of whom substitute descriptive terms for the details that would create a clearer image for readers. Instead of referring to a building as being *dilapidated,* specify the damage and neglect that lead you to describe it in that way. Keep in mind that your readers are diverse and that, for some, a building that needs painting is *dilapidated.* Others hear the term and picture cracked windows, a leaking roof and structural damage.

Height and weight generalizations, estimates of quantity and descriptions of quality pose similar problems in interpretation for writers and their readers.

How tall is "a tall man" to a reader who stands five feet six inches in height? Is that reader's "tall man" the same as the one pictured by a reader who is six feet tall?

How many people are actually in attendance at a funeral that you have described as having "many friends and relatives present"? Is the number the same as in those families that consider 30 people to be a crowd or 300 insufficient?

If you describe an individual as being "carelessly dressed," do you mean that the individual's clothing was dirty and wrinkled? Were the pieces mismatched? Was the clothing inappropriate to the occasion?

Never use generalizations in your writing, unless you want to leave interpretation of the information up to the reader. Instead, supply your readers with the details that led you to those generalizations to provide your readers with a clear and precise image of what you saw, heard, felt and thought.

ACTIVE RATHER THAN PASSIVE VOICE

Your choice of verb should relate the actor directly and swiftly to the action rather than reveal the connection in a roundabout manner. Passive voice verbs reverse the usual subject-verb-object sentence order and slow down a sentence because the subject is not the doer of the action.

Instead, events or results are identified before their causes. Something is being done to the subject, but who or what is performing that action is often unclear. In contrast, active voice verbs clearly tell the reader who is doing an action, and they move a sentence along at a swift pace. The following examples illustrate this difference.

Active: The students **carried** signs and **chanted** slogans to protest the tuition hike.

Passive: Signs **were carried** and slogans **were chanted** to protest the tuition hike.

Passive: Signs **were carried** and slogans **were chanted** by students to protest the tuition hike.

Active: The registrar's office **mailed** the grades for summer courses today.

Passive: The grades for summer courses **were mailed** today.

Passive: The grades for summer courses **were mailed** by the registrar's office today.

Active: Rescuers **found** only five survivors of the private jet crash.

Passive: Only five survivors of the private jet crash **were found.**

Passive: Only five survivors of the private jet crash **were found** by rescuers.

Read each trio of sentences aloud and *listen* to the different effect that the active voice produces. You know immediately who the actors are and what they did. Reading the first passive choice in each trio, you learn that something was done to the subject, but not who performed the action. The second passive choice in each group slows down the reader even further by adding a phrase to identify the actor in each instance. The passive sentences lack vitality.

Are there situations when the passive voice is appropriate in hard news or feature writing? Of course. Although you should use active verbs as frequently as possible, some situations make the passive voice mandatory.

Idiomatic expressions or common usage dictates the use of some passive verbs:

> Police **were called** to the scene.
> Their spirits **were dampened** by the rain.
> Court **was adjourned** until nine o'clock Tuesday morning.
> The dying man **was given** last rites.

The passive voice is also more appropriate in sentences that focus more on potential results than on who will achieve those results. In some cases, the subject may be truly unknown, yet the result is a key element in, if not the focus of, the story, so the passive voice is more appropriate.

> In case of civil disturbances, National Guard troops **are called** to quell an uprising.
> Plans to build a new field house on campus **have been deferred** until the projected state budget has passed.
> In our city, new council members **are elected** only if someone dies.

The passive voice is also useful as a means of removing yourself from a story, especially one based an interview or one observed in the making. When you have been a part of the action, the natural tendency is to fall into I narration, making such statements as "I asked the police captain if the building contained signs of forced entry" or "I watched the campus security staff disperse the crowd of angry, chanting students." The passive voice removes the writer from the story and places the emphasis where it should lie, on the subject of the article or interview.

> The police captain **was asked** if the building contained any signs of forced entry.
> The campus security staff **could be seen** dispersing the crowd of angry, chanting students.

There is another instance in which you may be required to use the passive voice—when interviewing bureaucrats. Listen carefully to any politician or representative of a government agency speak. Rarely does one take responsibility for an action or assign responsibility for an action to a specific committee or other unit of government. Thus, your interview with such an individual will likely be dominated by the passive voice. You will hear, and will have to echo, the following types of responses:

> The new policy governing campus parking was decided by the faculty-student senate.
> The fate of the bill was decided in a closed caucus.
> The antiabortion information was handed out by the agency.

By now, you may believe that the active and passive voices are divorced from each other, but they are not. Instances do exist in your writing in which both voices are needed to provide necessary variations in sound and rhythm. Even continuous brisk action can become boring and should be interrupted. Integrating passive verbs into a narrative serves as a means of breaking up the action and providing variety of expression. Examine the following paragraphs, which have only active voice verbs.

Students **arrive** at the stadium by 5 a.m. to buy tickets for the rock concert. The cold morning air **makes** some of them shiver. Some **wear** heavy coats and mufflers, and they **pull** their coats tightly around their bodies. All **focus** their eyes on the ticket window. They **carry** their money and credit cards in their pockets, ready for use.

Several people **pass** cigarettes to each other, and groups **huddle** together for warmth. Everyone **enjoys** the common experience. Security guards **keep** the crowd in line, but they **treat** the students in a friendly manner.

Everyone **stares** forward, waiting for the time to move quickly and the ticket window to open. When 9 a.m. **comes** and the tickets finally **go** on sale, relief **is felt** by both students and security. No violence **has occurred,** but the huge crowd **knows** that anything **could have happened** in that situation.

The passage contains only active verbs, making it move along fairly quickly but creating a somewhat terse tone. Because the subject matter is not tragic and the topic is not breaking news, a more relaxed tone is appropriate. To achieve that relaxed tone, the writer should infuse passive verbs at key points in the passage. Consider how the passage relaxes when some of the active verbs become passive.

Students **arrive** at the stadium by 5 a.m. to buy tickets for the rock concert. The cold morning air **makes** some of them shiver. Some **wear** mufflers and heavy coats, which **are pulled** tightly around their bodies. Their eyes **are focused** on the ticket window, and their money and credit cards **are lying** in their pockets, ready for use.

Cigarettes **are passed** around as groups **huddle** together for warmth. Everyone **enjoys** the common experience. Security guards **keep** the crowd in line, but the students **are treated** in a friendly manner.

Everyone **stares** forward, waiting for the time to move quickly and the ticket window to open. When 9 a.m. **comes** and the tickets finally **go** on sale, relief **is felt** by both students and security guards. No violence **has occurred,** but the huge crowd **knows** that anything **could have happened** in that situation.

Changing five of the 16 active verbs to passive verbs changes the tone of the passage and eliminates the repetitive sound and rhythm created by the exclusive use of active verbs. By dispersing the passive verbs throughout the passage, the writer improves the flow of the language and alters the pace of the story.

USAGE

Writing for a newspaper or a magazine requires that you use standard English. Many writers do not realize that contractions and colloquialisms are informal English. As such, they should be eliminated from your writing unless you use them in quoting subjects of interviews.

You know that contractions are combinations of two words to form a third word, one that contains an apostrophe to replace missing letters.

Some writers habitually—and inappropriately—contract subjects and verbs, writing *he's* for *he is* or *he has*. Others frequently use more familiar contractions in their writing, such as *can't, won't, it's, shouldn't* and others. If a contraction is part of a phrase that commonly appears in writing, use it. The caution is against the excessive use of contractions throughout your writing.

Colloquialisms are created words that have become part of conversation. Many are shorter versions of existing words. Instead of *photos, reps, reverb* or *recap,* use the complete version of each word in your writing: *photographs, representatives, reverberation* and *recapitulation.*

Other usage errors are the result of a confusion that writers should take the time to correct. The argument of some writers that readers will probably not know the difference between correct and incorrect usage is inexcusable. Learn the difference between commonly confused words and eliminate frequent errors in usage now. The following are the most common mistakes cited by editors.

- **affect, effect.** *Affect* is more frequently used as a verb.

Example:

His behavior will affect the outcome of the game.
Effect is more frequently used as a noun.

Example:

What will be the effect of your actions on the game?
Both words can also play other roles. *Affect* can function as a noun, but its use is largely confined to psychological literature.

Example:

The study will measure *affect* following treatment with the drug.
Effect can function as a verb meaning to bring about.

Example:

Researchers have learned that chocolate can effect change in some personality types.

- **allude, refer.** To *allude* means to hint at something without mentioning it directly. To *refer* means to mention directly.

- **among, between.** Use the preposition *among* when comparing or introducing more than two of anything. Use *between* when only two items are involved.
- **because, since.** Use *because* to establish a cause-effect relationship. Despite the growing casual use of *since* to substitute for *because,* resist the trend and use *since* to establish a time frame.

Example:

The police left because the crowd had dispersed.

Example:

A long time has passed since the founding of the village.

- **blond, blonde; brunet, brunette; fiance, fiancee.** Use the first term in each pair to refer to males, and the second term to refer to females. The difference is due to the French origin of the words in which an *e* is added to an adjective when it modifies a feminine noun.
- **boy, girl.** Use these terms for the appropriate sex of individuals under the age of 18. Individuals over the age of 18 become *young man* or *man* and *young woman* or *woman.*
- **compare to, compare with.** To compare two items that are unlike, use *compare to.* To compare similar items, use *compare with.*
- **either.** *Either* should be used to mean one or the other. Many writers mistakenly use the term to mean both, as in "the chairs were placed on either side of the stage."
- **farther, further.** Use *farther* to speak of physical distance. Use *further* in relation to time or degree of something.

Example:

The farther I walk, the more tired I become.

Example:

The mayor will examine the issue further.

- **fewer, less.** When enumerating individual items, use *fewer.* Use *less* for references to quantity.

Example:

Fewer people attended the meeting tonight than last week.

Example:

The city collected less garbage this year than in previous years.

- **good, well.** Use *good* as an adjective meaning something pleasing or better than average. Use *well* as an adjective only when referring to health. You may also use *well* as an adverb to describe something accomplished in a satisfactory manner.
- **imply, infer.** View the difference between *imply* and *infer* as comparable to the difference between transmitting and receiving information.

Example:

Your writing may imply information from which the readers will infer meaning.

- **in, into.** Use *in* to indicate location and *into* to indicate motion.

Example:

The lawyers are in the judge's chambers.

Example:

The lawyers walked into the judge's chambers.

- **lay, lie.** Use forms of the verb *lay* to indicate action and to substitute for the verb *to place.* Use *lie* to indicate a state of reclining.

Example:

We will lay the wreaths on the graves.

Example:

The protesters will lie in the street to protest the new highway.

- **majority, plurality.** Use *majority* when referring to more than half of a number. Use *plurality* when referring to the highest among several numbers.

Example:

With 51 votes, James received the majority of the 100 votes cast.

Example:

With 44 votes, Clinton received a plurality of the 100 votes cast, beating Harding's 32 and Ryan's 24.

- **over, more than.** The two terms are not interchangable. Use *over* to provide spatial information. Use *more than* to enumerate items or people.

Example:

The blimp hovered over Giants' Stadium.

Example:

The police reported more than 50 arrests.

- **who, whom.** *Who* is the subjective form of the pronoun and should be used to replace the subject of a sentence, clause or phrase. *Whom* is the objective form of the pronoun and should be used as the object of a verb or a preposition.
- **widow, widower.** A *widower* is a man whose wife dies, and a *widow* is a woman whose husband dies. Avoid redundancy by writing about "the widower of the late ___."

BIAS-FREE LANGUAGE

Increased attention to political correctness in language has become a concern on all levels of society and in all areas of communication. The writer who makes the mistake of assuming the correct term to describe a racial, ethnic, age, disability or other group without asking a member of that advocacy group may offend many individuals. To avoid this problem, take the time to develop a list of people and groups whom you can call to check terminology. Even if you feel embarrassed, ask the people about whom you are writing what they prefer to be called.

Terms that may seem to be in general use may actually be offensive to your subject. A good example is the term *Hispanic,* which is broadly applied to Spanish-speaking people from a wide range of areas. Most individuals would prefer to be viewed as individuals. If you have taken the time to include a person in your story, then take the time to ask about that person's country of origin. Those born in Puerto Rico, Peru, Cuba and Ecuador prefer to be distinguished from each other and from people born in Venezuela, Colombia, the Dominican Republic and other nations in which Spanish is the official language.

Other racial and ethnic groups also prefer a writer to ask their preferences in designation. *Native Americans* prefer not to be confused with individuals born in India. People born in Haiti prefer to be described as *Haitian-Americans* rather than lumped under the general racial term of *African-Americans.* Someone of Serbian, Bosnian, Macedonian or Croatian descent would feel insulted to be grouped under the now-outdated term *Yugoslavian.*

Be sensitive to the feelings of people who have mental or physical disabilities. They are not "disabled people," but they are people first, and their disabilities are a secondary aspect. Thus, your subjects, when the reference is appropriate, are "people who are visually impaired," "people who are deaf," "people with mental retardation" or "people with emotional disorders." Avoid making the physical limitations of a person a major part of the story *unless* that is the story. Such references in stories that are not at all connected to disabilities are condescending.

References to age should avoid all mention of stereotypical characteristics, such as "gray-haired," "senior citizen," "old" or "rocking chair bound." Include a person's age if it is relevant in the story, but do not use age as a means of heightening the sense of wonder at the person's accomplishments. Readers can make the judgment, if they want, to react with surprise if a 70-year-old man wins a swimming competition that includes many younger individuals. To focus on age creates what some editors call the "gee whiz" or "golly" tone in an article. The writer emerges sounding naive.

Sexism in language can also be corrected. Writers should not automatically use masculine pronouns to refer to non-sex-specific nouns, such as student, teacher or writer. Correct the error by making the noun plural and use the plural pronoun reference. Eliminate all words that start or end with *man* and replace the term with a word that more fully describes the function of that individual. Rather than "fireman" use "firefighter," for "mailman" use "mail carrier," and for "Congressman" use "member of Congress."

Strike stereotypes when speaking of men and women. Some women might protest that they are not insulted by such terms as "old wives' tale," "throwing like a girl" or "mothering instinct," but many prefer the terms "fallacies," "pitch poorly" and "nurturing instinct."

Be careful of the adjectives that you use to describe the women about whom you write. Consider whether you would use the same terms in a profile of a man. Sexual attributes have no place in a story about an individual's business, educational or other professional activities. If you would not refer to the male president of a major corporation as having a "seductive smile," why would any writer use that term to describe a woman in a similar position?

One final difference in news style references to men and women has been eradicated in recent years. In the past, first names were used to refer to women, and last names were used for men. Contemporary style demands that last names be used to refer to both.

The issue of political correctness is not as complicated as some make it seem. You appreciate others treating you as an individual and being sensitive to your preferences—simply return the favor. Ask your subjects how they wish to be designated, and use the terms that they prefer. One caution, however, because you may not feel fully comfortable with a term even after consulting a group or an individual: protect your image by stating in the article that the individual has specified the term.

Chapter Seven

Description: Creating Images for Readers

Description enables a writer to convey images, evoke emotion and introduce innuendo into what might otherwise remain a list of dry facts. With vivid detail and specific imagery, the writer of interesting prose will show, not tell, the reader about a person, incident or location. To obtain material to create the type of description that will maintain reader interest, you have to become highly observant and record even the most minute details. Instead of merely recording them, however, you must devise connections between these details and your subject. You must also be highly selective in deciding which details to include in an article—and which to omit.

BECOMING A TRAINED OBSERVER

A good writer is a trained observer, a person whose senses are always alert to the sights, sounds, smells, feelings and tastes of the surrounding world. Even when no story is lurking in the background, most writers continually gather material and store details in memory.

Many writers carry a notebook wherever they go, because they know that everything in life has the potential to become a story. They make notations unobtrusively, mentally filing away information for potential use. The odd family connection, the intriguing name, the appearance of a celebrity at a public or private gathering—no one can tell when a future story might benefit from information recorded in the present, at a time when there is no apparent need for such information.

Writers for newspapers and magazines, both hard news and feature, use description to enrich their work and to make it come alive for readers. Less description may appear in the hard news article, which seeks mainly to report the facts—little more than the *who, what, when, where, why,* and *how* of a story. This limitation does not mean that news articles do not contain description, because they do. The difference is in the amount. The tight construction of the hard news style benefits from the inclusion of a select number of well-chosen descriptive details that supplement but do not dominate the writing.

Description should not be mistakenly viewed as being padding or filler material in either a hard news or a feature article. Writers who include description simply to fill space in either type of article usually do not see their work reach publication, or they must accept severe editing of the content. Although more extensive detail is desirable in feature writing, wasteful words that simply take up space on the page are the first to go.

Avoid the mistake of thinking that description consists of merely accumulating adjectives or adverbs. These modifiers are useful, but they represent a minor technique in the valuable art of using description well. Adjectives and adverbs *tell* readers about a subject. Specific details *show* readers. Consider the following examples.

Example 1:

City Fire Company No. 4 was called yesterday to the site of an abandoned garage on Maple Street, where firefighters found a cat rescuing her kittens from the burning building.

The animals were taken to County Animal Shelter, where they were treated for smoke inhalation. The mother cat, given the name Scarlett by firefighters, was treated also for severe burns.

The shelter has received over 300 calls from people who wish to adopt Scarlett and the surviving four kittens.

Example 2:

The fur is singed from the left side of her head, the eye is swollen closed, and her badly burned paws are bandaged. She breathes heavily as she sleeps in her cage at the shelter, an exhausted mother with four kittens pressed close to her side.

Her one good eye opens occasionally, when a tiny shoulder or paw pokes hard against the raw, burned skin on her side. The five do not seem to have adjusted to their decreased number, because they leave just enough space for one more kitten to snuggle close to the brave mother cat.

Today, the five are recovering from their fiery ordeal yesterday. Responding to a call to put out a fire in an abandoned garage, firefighters were surprised to see the mother cat, whom they have named Scarlett, running out of the burning building and across the street with what appeared to be a scrap of fur in her mouth. She returned four times to the burning building. Sparks flew from burning beams, and the billowing black smoke poured out of cracks in the walls, as firefighters feared that the roof would collapse. On her last trip, she must have been hit by burning rubble, because she limped and fur was burned from her left side, but her jaws held firm.

Once all five kittens were with her, Scarlett inspected them with her tongue, cleaning them roughly until they cried. Only one kitten lay still, too weak to whimper. He died of smoke inhalation soon after the six animals reached County Animal Shelter.

The shelter has received over 300 calls from people touched by Scarlett's bravery and offering to adopt her and the kittens.

Which of the preceding accounts would you prefer to read? The first account tells you that Scarlett and her kittens escaped from a fire. How they escaped and what role Scarlett played are not embellished. This account also tells you that she suffered burns and that they all suffered from smoke inhalation. Thus, you have facts—and little more.

The second account provides the descriptive details to *show* why Scarlett is of greater interest than the first account indicates. To rescue her kittens, she had to endanger herself four times after initially escaping from the burning building. She suffered injury and burns, yet her mission was to save the kittens with no apparent thought to her own safety. The second account provides details that show the reader how frightening the circumstances must have been, with sparks flying, smoke pouring out of the building, and burning debris falling. Her determination is also shown in her final trip out, as she limps and appears to be seriously hurt, yet she holds the last kitten firmly in her jaws.

A story of this sort evokes compassion in most readers without the need for evocative details to touch their emotions. The second account is not needed to stir compassion, but the descriptive details do make Scarlett's ordeal come alive for readers, and the details produce a more interesting and enjoyable article. To be blunt, the first account has the potential to evoke a "so what?" response from some readers who fail to see the importance of a story about cats at the scene of a fire.

This description can serve several purposes for a writer. The story of Scarlett's bravery might be a good stand-alone feature article, or it might become part of a larger article that focuses on the instincts, rights or parenting abilities of animals in general or cats in particular. Taking a different approach, the vividly detailed description of the ordeal suffered by Scarlett and her kittens might also become a valuable example to include in an article on the subject of fire safety, the dangers of abandoned buildings or the response of callers to the shelter.

Depending on the emphasis of the eventual story, the writer can increase or decrease the descriptive details to suit the theme. Either way, a large pool of details should be created, even if more than half of the observations must be omitted before publication.

USING DESCRIPTION IN THE HARD NEWS ARTICLE

What type of descriptive detail *is* valuable in a hard news article? The requirements may vary according to the subject of the article, but one point is consistent: the writer must be present and personally record the details. How else can you represent them as your observations?

Always write down every observation that you believe is even slightly important, and use precise language in your notes. Mannerisms and details of physical appearance may seem to be clear and committed to memory, but even a brief time away from the subject can make sharp details fade.

To illustrate how description fits into the hard news article, consider a story that reports an auto accident. The facts of the story may be the following:

Who: John Smith and Jane Doe
What: Automobile collision; one injury
When: Yesterday at 4 p.m.
Where: Corner of Hazel Street and Elm Avenue
Why: Drivers claimed poor visibility
How: Car driven by Doe northbound on Hazel and turning right onto Elm; car driven by Smith eastbound on Elm.

These facts combined into a summary lead provide readers with the facts of the accident. The paragraphs that follow the lead should then supply additional information that will maintain the interest of those who continue to read.

> Police and emergency medical personnel responded yesterday to an automobile collision at the corner of Hazel Street and Elm Avenue, which involved John Smith and Jane Doe, both of the city.

What type of description does this hard news article require? Are physical descriptions of Doe and Smith important? Are their ages important to the story? What about their heights or what they were wearing? Who was injured and how badly?

No one but the writer can decide which descriptive details are important enough to include and which to ignore. That decision must be made on a story-by-story basis. To make those determinations, the writer must be on the scene.

Many seemingly odd incidents become news stories, and the circumstances of the incident determine how much and what type of description to include.

Suppose that the John Smith of this story is a seven-year-old boy who had often watched his parents drive the family car. Even though he is so short that he cannot see over the steering wheel and he can barely reach the gas pedal, he decides to take the keys and drive away with the car. Are his age and height important to the story? Should the writer include a brief physical description of him? Of course, you should include that information because it is an integral part of this specific incident. Also include a description of his attitude when the police arrive. Is he frightened, dazed, belligerent?

Now consider some possibilities for Jane Doe. Perhaps she is wearing a loose-fitting cardigan sweater with roomy sleeves that flare at the wrists. She might have reached to downshift and caught her sleeve on the shift knob. The resulting movement to free herself might prevent the wheel from turning sufficiently to clear Smith's car in the turn. Is a brief description of the sweater important? It is in this case because the item appears to have contributed to the accident.

The examples given here are not as far-fetched as you may think. Newspaper articles have identified far stranger reasons for automobile collisions—and all of them benefit from description, however brief.

Which senses should the writer use in recording observations at the scene? The obvious answer is "all of them," but the reality is that not all stories call upon all five of the writer's senses. Some stories provide the opportunity to use only sight, others employ sound and smell, and still others call for additional combinations.

Visual details are most important in a news story about a two-car collision. Describe the condition of the cars. If only the front of each car is damaged in the accident, observe the overall condition of the cars. Are they well kept? Is either car new? Is only one car badly damaged? Are both cars badly damaged? What is damaged on each?

To decide which details are important, the writer has to determine if the story ends with the facts recorded in the summary lead, or if something else happens at the scene. Does either car begin leaking fluids onto the street? Is fire a risk? Are any buildings in the area damaged? Are bystanders involved? Does either car contain passengers? Is anything noteworthy about either car? Is anything noteworthy about the location? Is anything noteworthy about either driver?

Describe the street and sidewalk at the intersection where the accident occurred. Is broken glass lying on the street? Have light covers fallen off?

Use yourself as a measure to determine the need for observation. Any question that evokes your interest as a writer should lead you to a more careful observation and a detailed on-the-scene description.

The hard news article presents a challenge because many questions such as those listed here cannot be recollected and answered in tranquillity. The writer has to have the presence of mind to consider the possibilities and to note immediately as many details as possible at the scene. Beginning writers frequently find such preparation to be daunting, but as they gain experience, they become adept at applying certain set questions to hard news situations.

USING DESCRIPTION IN THE FEATURE ARTICLE

Feature articles offer writers a greater opportunity to include descriptive detail than do hard news articles, because the greater length eliminates the time and subject restrictions. Profiles of noteworthy people, human interest stories, self-help articles, and entertaining and inspirational stories depend on description to make readers become a part of the story.

Because descriptive detail emerges from observation, the responsibility for the success or failure of this effort lies solely with the writer. A dull and boring subject does not have to becomes a dull and boring article. Every topic is a challenge, from determining how to approach the subject to deciding what to include or omit. The less interesting subject simply calls upon more of a writer's skills and talent of observation—and the way in which observation reveals descriptive details.

Review several celebrity profiles in large-circulation newspapers or well-known magazines. Observe that the writer might begin with a brief physical word sketch of the subject, but the greater part of the description unfolds throughout the writing.

What if you are asked to write a profile of a local politician who is currently running? Do you begin with a physical description, followed by a modified resume of education and experience in public office? Do you ask the subject her views regarding the issues which she has been known to support, and then report them verbatim?

If you handle the profile in this manner, your article will be informative, but it might not be read beyond the first few paragraphs. Inexperienced writers *tell* readers details about a subject, but the experienced writer *shows* readers.

A lively article that will interest readers provides descriptions of the subject's behavior and relates incidents that show the subject's private side and views. Consider the following examples, one which presents a paragraph from a story with a mainly factual format, and the other that draws upon sensory details for description.

Example 1:

Jane Smith has served for three years on the city council, in addition to her one year as deputy mayor. She asserts that her graduate degree in business and management has guided her to make decisions that have saved the city nearly a million dollars in the past year. When asked how this experience would be useful in her role as mayor, she points to the computer on her desk and says, "This city is run by politicians my age, and many of them are computer-illiterate. They do not realize how important a city networking tool computers are, nor how much money we can save the people by installing special accounting systems and other software in city hall to eliminate duplication of labor."

Example 2:

Jane Smith conveys an air of polished efficiency in her expensively furnished office that contains eight locked black file cabinets, each of the 32 drawers neatly identified with a coded label. Books stand upright on the polished oak shelves, organized first according to topic, then alphabetically. The supply cabinet contains an inventory list on the front, which her assistant is expected to update at the end of each workday. Her computer and other desktop equipment are all exactly placed inside their appropriate markings on the desk. She explains that she has taken this precaution, at the risk of defacing the wood surface, so that cleaning and repair people can return the equipment to the arrangements that she has found most comfortable. Smith sits stiffly upright in the expensive leather executive desk chair throughout the interview, not once leaning against the comfortable-appearing tufted back nor forward to rest her arms on the desk.

The descriptive details create a much clearer profile of Jane Smith than her own words. The feeling that Smith has a place for everything and that everything is in its place emerges in the organization of the books and supply cabinet, as well as in the markings on her desk to keep all of her equipment lined up as she wants it to be. The details also promote the image of a very controlling personality that seems unwilling to relinquish control in any area. The examples are much more effective than any expressions by the subject could be.

OMITTING DETAILS

Not every observation made by a writer deserves a place in the final article. As you must narrow the focus of a subject, you must also limit the number of details included. Consider the excerpt just presented from a profile of politician Jane Smith. While the writer sat in Smith's office, she also noticed details about Smith's hairstyle, makeup, manicure and other grooming concerns. The old building in which Smith's office is located has an old heating system, so the radiators occasionally let out a hiss, and banging sounded at intervals as the hot water coursed through the pipes. Paint is peeling from the ceiling, 20 feet high, and the tiled floor shows extensive wear.

Some of these details might improve the article, depending on the writer's focus, but not all of what has appeared can be added to the sample paragraph if the writer wants to maintain the existing focus. Descriptive details that do not advance the author's purpose should be omitted.

Chapter Eight

Using Quotations Wisely

Direct quotations can spice up your writing and make readers acutely aware of the real people behind the events recounted in your writing. Applied with too heavy a hand, however, quotations can ruin an article.

The difference lies in knowing what makes a good quote.

WHY USE QUOTATIONS?

Not every word of an interview is valuable. Nor is every statement made by the people whom you interview. You may have to sort through thousands of boring, mundane, redundant and useless words to find one good direct quote. That is time well spent, because the right quote will perform magic by making a personal connection between your readers and your subject.

Be selective and do not overload your writing with quotations. The deadly repetition of "he said," "said she," "she says" and "says she" is one reason for using restraint. The more important reason to limit the number of quotations is that an article filled with them is nothing more than a question-and-answer interview that shows no talent and little effort on your part. The writer who leans too heavily on quotations functions hardly more than a recorder of the subject's observations. That is not a writer's function.

What can quotations do for your writing? Quotations are similar to description in their ability to make writing come alive. A person's words invoke for readers the image of an individual who has a real story to tell. The professional writer is always suspect when relating someone else's story. Readers know that you are paid for the writing, so an unspoken distrust of your motives always exists at some level. When you quote the subject, however, much of that distrust dissipates.

Quotations serve several valuable functions, but they should not be used as crutches. Good quotations will not make up for bad writing, so make certain that the framework of the article is sound before looking for quotations that will enhance an already strong discussion.

- Use quotations to provide a punch line—a pithy statement that sums up lengthy explanations.
- Use quotations to offer a counterpoint to discussion of a specific point.
- Use quotations to show the agreement *or* disagreement of someone important.
- Use quotations to introduce a unique perspective.

CHOOSING EFFECTIVE QUOTATIONS

What should you look for in quotations? Choose direct quotations carefully. Do not waste space with quotations that contain statistics, technical information, background material or facts. Present such material in your own words, condensing and paraphrasing the information as needed. Give credit to the source of this material as part of the text, but do not waste the power of the direct quote on such ordinary content.

Consider the difference in impact between these two methods—the direct quote and the paraphrase—in the following examples.

Example 1:

"Construction on the power plant should begin in July," says Mayor Tomlin. "The project will create 40 new jobs in the city and take eight months to complete. I am very happy to be mayor at a time when we will experience this boon to the economy."

Example 2:

> Power plant construction will begin in July and continue for eight months, according to Mayor Tomlin, who estimates that the project will create 40 new jobs.

The information in the mayor's quote is important to the city economy, and to his status as a city official, but his exact words reveal nothing about him, nor do they provide any insights into his thinking beyond what appears. So why quote him?

Your paraphrase of this information makes the material blend with the style of the article and eliminates useless words. If you were to place this quote into a hard news article, you would miss the opportunity to combine the preceding details with additional information about the project. Even less use could be made of the quote in a soft news or feature article.

Be brutal in differentiating between those quotations that have possibilities for inclusion in your article and those that should be either struck entirely or combined into a well-written paraphrase. Resist the urge to include a statement simply because the subject emphasized the information or made a particular point to ensure that you took down every word accurately.

A direct quote should contain only the words of the speaker, verbatim, with no interpolation by the writer in most instances. News style does allow writers to correct grammar in the statements of an individual who made the error in speech but might correct the error in writing. In contrast, if regionalisms and incorrect grammar are characteristic of the individual, leave the errors in the statement to convey a sense of authenticity.

When an article carries your byline, you are responsible for the content, as well as for the expression of that content. You decide which words are vital and which are disposable. Do so with a vengeance before submitting an article. An editor will gladly slash useless or ineffective quotations from your writing, but leaving that work to someone else will also decrease your status as a dependable and competent writer.

How do you know whether a quote is worth using in an article? Ask *yourself* several questions about the material, and use your answers to determine whether a quote stays or goes.

- Does the quote add color or credibility to the article?
- Is the quote unique in content?
- Is the quote unique in expression?
- Does the quote reveal a secret or a hidden agenda?
- Does the quote reveal the speaker's personal beliefs?
- Does the quote reveal obscure motives for an action?
- Does the quote reveal the speaker's ignorance?
- Is the quote uncharacteristically passionate?
- Does the quote reveal the inner subject as opposed to the public facade?
- Overall, does the quote provide readers with a unique perspective and information about the speaker that is expressed best in the quote?

INTEGRATING QUOTATIONS INTO TEXT

An article must maintain a consistent tone throughout, and the quotations that you use should reflect this tone. Selecting quotations for shock value can be counterproductive because readers quickly become jaded by exclamations and outrageous opinions that appear frequently in the text. The quotations you use must be strongly related to the story, or they become useless diversions that confuse readers and draw them away from your intentions.

Using Quotations in the Lead
Quotations may appear early in an article to set the tone and to provide a clear indication of the writer's proposed direction. The hard news lead requires a significant quote to quickly convey relevant information and opinions. You should quote only someone involved in the story or someone important.

In an article about the demonstration of Montcalm State University students against a state-mandated tuition hike, several perspectives may be followed in different articles about that event. Each perspective is signaled by the quote used to open the article.

> "Many students will be unable to attend college because of the financial hardship that the 25% state-mandated tuition increase creates," said Montcalm State University president Aaron Christian, who supported the Wednesday protest during which students demonstrated and blocked the entrance to the student union building.

(The article will be a hard news focus on the "official" college administrator's view of this increase and its financial implications.)

> "It is time that students in this state stopped getting a free ride and started to pay their way," says E. B. Scrooge, a state legislator who voted for the increase.

(The article will be a hard news focus on the cost-cutting measures related to education that underlie the legislature's decision.)

> "At least six of my friends and I will probably have to leave college because we can't afford the increase," says Donna Marie, a sophomore at Montcalm State University.

(The article could either take a hard news focus or develop into a news feature that will examine the effect that the increase will have on a range of students at the university.)

Quotations that open an article are the most difficult to select. Alienate your readers at that point, and you have lost them for good. Intrigue readers, and they will continue to read.

The opening passage from an article about late American poet Allen Ginsberg, used in Chapter Four as one example of how writers might organize paragraphs, is very useful in examining the manner in which quotations appearing at the beginning of a work influence readers' expectations for the article. The 201 words presented here are part of a much longer piece that runs to approximately 3,000 words and contains additional quotations placed at select points in the text.

Few people met the legendary poet Allen Ginsberg and walked away unchanged by the experience. He was a man who impressed others by his mere presence.

"I only met him once," says one middle-aged woman, "but his kindness and wisdom are forever in my memory."

"He was a radical hippie who rocked society, and then was rewarded by the very society he sneered at," says a former Brooklyn College student of his. "I admire that."

Raised in Paterson, New Jersey, in a culturally and politically mixed environment, Allen Ginsberg sought to relate to all people. His political views were radically liberal, yet he was an advocate for peace, not violent revolution. He embraced Buddhism yet retained much of his Jewish heritage.

Newspapers of the 1960s recorded his opposition to the war in Vietnam. Photographs showed him slipping the stems of daffodils into the rifle barrels of National Guardsmen sent to disperse demonstrators. He often spoke out against the war at public gatherings, and his poems contained antiwar fervor.

Ginsberg became a target of the FBI because of his political activities. Then-Director J. Edgar Hoover ordered agents to gather information about the poet's activities. The eventual file ran to several thousand pages.

How do the quotations function in this article? The first point to note is that neither speaker is named because the article is about Ginsberg. Our interest in these two people is limited to their observations about and connections to the subject. In this approach, the speakers' words may reveal their feelings and beliefs, but their names are insignificant to readers who care only how those thoughts and feelings relate to the late poet.

Several important lessons about using direct quotations appear in this example. Each speaker presents a different perspective on the same man, thus creating a mandate for the writer to address those differing perspectives in the article. The issue of attribution, discussed later in this chapter, is also important. Pay close attention both to the writer's choice of speakers and to their words.

Readers who know that Ginsberg (1926–1997) was an outspoken opponent of the Vietnam War in the 1960s and 1970s realize that the "middle-aged woman" who praises Ginsberg's "kindness and wisdom" was a college student during the poet's most actively radical period. She probably formed her impressions of him at about the same age as the second speaker, a former college student of his.

The contrast between their responses to the man provide the writer with numerous possibilities for development in the article. Some of these possibilities follow in the paragraphs that make up the article lead. The writer incorporates similar contrasts in condensing material related to the poet's life. The material relates to both the "kindness and wisdom" perceived by the first speaker and the "radical hippie who rocked" and "sneered at" society perceived by the second speaker. In short, the contrasting quotations, observed by seemingly different individuals, establish a pattern of contrasting views that should continue throughout the article.

Using Quotations in the Body of the Article

The writer must choose quotations carefully, whether they are placed in the opening of the article or dispersed throughout the body. The quotations used in the body are easier to select because they are chosen to become part of a theme and pattern that have already been established in the lead. Therefore, sorting out irrelevant quotations becomes easier.

What may seem to be an effortless use of quotations is usually a carefully planned pattern in which the writer has plotted the appearance and effect of each quote. One effective pattern depends on an alternation of quotations with the writer's material throughout the article. The length of the material between the quotations varies according to the length of the article, but selectivity still determines how many quotations are used.

This pattern may begin with a quote. The writer then follows with a paraphrase, summary or description that the quote illustrates. The material that follows the quote should not summarize or explain the quote. The point is to inform readers—not bore them—so choose quotations that are lively and interesting.

This pattern may also be reversed. The writer might first present the paraphrase, summary or description, and then use a quote that supports or illustrates the argument contained in the material.

The lead to the Ginsberg article is a good example of the way in which both patterns work. The opening sentence generalizes about Ginsberg's life, and the two quotations each illustrate the manner in which the speakers were impressed by the man. The quotations *then* function as catalysts for the ideas that the writer will develop further by describing and summing up Ginsberg's activities. As the article continues, quotations will alternate with lengthy passages of the writer's text.

ATTRIBUTING QUOTATIONS

Attribution simply means to give credit to the person whose quote you use or, in the view of some writers, to give blame. Read carefully through several hard news articles, and you will find that most do associate a speaker with the quotations, but not all do. The practice of attributing information to "an unnamed source" or to "a bureau spokesperson who prefers to remain anonymous" is still in use, but many large-circulation papers deride the practice. Their view is that information from a person who refuses to be named may not be fully accurate. Another fear is that the writer may have made up the quote. If you want to use information but cannot attribute it to a specific individual, avoid the direct quote and paraphrase the material instead.

Another observation to make while scanning newspapers is the manner in which the attribution is handled. You have been told repeatedly to use strong verbs (as discussed in Chapter Six) and to be precise in language so that you can convey an exact message to readers. Attribution requires an exception to that rule.

A quote should be well chosen to provide life, meaning, credibility, poignancy or another effect to writing. Why undermine the planned effect by using a competing verb in the attribution? News style refrains from using distracting verbs, such as "he bellowed" or "she shouted," and uses the simple "she says," "she said," "he says," "he said," and so on. Feature articles may exhibit greater leeway in the choice of attribution verbs, but the smart writer takes a hard look at the effect that the chosen verb will have on the quote before rejecting "she says." The desire to show cleverness in this area is not worth the risk of draining the power from a quote.

Where is the best placement for the attribution? The value of a skillful attribution is that it provides needed information yet appears invisible. The writer should make clear to readers the identity of the speaker as early as possible in the quote. At the same time, an attribution should not interrupt the flow of the writing, nor should it dominate the quote.

Where the attribution appears—before the quote, in the middle, at the end—depends on the specific quote.

- In quotations of more than one sentence, place the attribution at the end of the first sentence.

Example:

> "He took our dignity first," says union representative James Ellis. "Now he wants to take our jobs."

- If the quote is only one sentence, place the attribution at a point where the speaker pauses naturally to take a breath, and then continue with the quote.

Example:

> "Few regrets are as great," says Raima Rhodes, "as the emotional cost of not taking an active role in your children's childhood."

- If the quote is short or contains no natural pause, begin with the attribution.

Example:

> School board president John Brown said, "We are going to weed out all of the incompetent school administrators."

- The least desirable place for an attribution is after the entire quote. If the quote is carefully chosen, it will probably build to increased emphasis at the end. When this is the case, the end attribution actually destroys the dramatic force of the quote.

Example:

> "The only thing we have to fear is fear itself," said President Franklin Delano Roosevelt in his first inaugural address.

How much is enough when using quotations? Read the article aloud, but omit your writing. If the quotations alone tell the story, then the article depends too heavily upon the words of the subject or sources. Revise the material by providing more of your own assessment and conclusions, punctuated—not dominated—by quotations.

Chapter Nine

Ending the Article Successfully

The greatest difference between hard news and feature articles is the nature of their endings. The writers of hard news articles do not worry too much about this and usually end their articles when they have completed presenting information. In contrast, the feature article, usually longer in word count than the hard news story, must provide the reader with closure, by providing a definite ending that clearly completes the discussion that the writer promises in the lead. In brief, the ending of the feature article has to remain so compelling that the reader will continue to the end and the editor will be unable to remove it.

ENDING THE HARD NEWS ARTICLE

The article that follows standard news style is constructed in the inverted pyramid format, which places the most important material in the first few paragraphs. The summary lead is followed by supporting paragraphs that contain information arranged in descending order of importance.

The writer knows that the editor of the hard news article will begin at the bottom to shorten the material, making the ending the first part to go. The reality is that writers have no reason to invest too much time and effort in rounding out the article with a carefully constructed ending. Despite the possibility that the ending will vanish before the article is published, a writer should still write the ending and complete the work.

Hard news article endings depend on the focus of the story. Recall the variations on the summary leads that appear in Chapter Three. The same basic information appears in each, but the *arrangement* of the information creates a different focus for the article, as well as for readers. The ending must support this focus. You can just end the article when you have nothing more to write and reach a cutoff point. A more effective ending shows effort and may include a *quote*, a *future action* or another *fact*.

Review the following summary leads, all written to begin a hard news article about a student demonstration at Montcalm State University. Each focus points toward a different ending.

Summary Lead 1—Emphasis on *Who*

Students at Montcalm State University demonstrated by carrying signs and blocking the entrance to the student union building on Wednesday to protest a state-mandated tuition increase scheduled to take effect in September 1998.

Possible Ending

Students present at the demonstration have already set a date for a follow-up demonstration, in which they will be joined by faculty who have already pledged their support.

Summary Lead 2—Emphasis on *What*

A protest against the state-mandated tuition increase scheduled to take effect in September 1998 was staged on Wednesday at Montcalm State University by students who demonstrated by carrying signs and blocking the entrance to the student union building.

Possible Ending

This has been the first time in 23 years that students at the university have faced an issue that united so many diverse members of the campus community.

Summary Lead 3—Emphasis on *When*

On Wednesday, students at Montcalm State University demonstrated by carrying signs and blocking the entrance to the student union building to protest the state-mandated tuition increase scheduled to take effect in September 1998.

Possible Ending

Campus security chief James Gold, impressed by the orderly nature of the demonstration, said, "Students know that many of us support their effort, and they showed us the courtesy of not making our already difficult job harder."

Summary Lead 4—Emphasis on *Where*

At Montcalm State University on Wednesday, students protested the state-mandated tuition increase, scheduled to take effect in September 1998, by demonstrating with signs and blocking the entrance to the student union building.

Possible Ending

Demonstrations at the other state colleges and universities are expected throughout the next two weeks.

Summary Lead 5—Emphasis on *Why*

To protest the state-mandated tuition increase scheduled to take effect in September 1998, students at Montcalm State University demonstrated by carrying signs on Wednesday and blocking the entrance to the student union building.

Possible Ending

After noting the extensive media coverage of the demonstration, student leader Ann Smith said, "I hope that the governor and the legislature get the message and realize that we are also voters, or soon to be."

Summary Lead 6—Emphasis on *How*

By demonstrating with signs and blocking the entrance to the student union building on Wednesday, students at Montcalm State University staged a protest against the state-mandated tuition increase scheduled to take effect in September 1998.

Possible Ending

Plans for the next demonstration will extend student efforts to additional locations on the campus.

The six summary leads make use of all three possible endings to hard news articles. Summary leads 1 and 6 end with news of a future action, while Summary leads 2 an 4 offer facts related to the occurrence described in the present article. Summary leads 3 and 5 end with quotes, and the writers have been careful to place the attributions preceding each quote.

ENDING THE FEATURE ARTICLE

Writers of feature articles develop their stories in ways that are significantly different from the hard news approach. Because the feature article goes beyond the goal of merely informing readers, such articles also take more time to engage the reader in the topic. The ending must be consistent with this goal and keep the reader interested to the very end, if the writer is to achieve the ultimate impact.

The lead and the ending of the feature article must function as a partnership, a joint effort that shows the reader where you are headed and where you have arrived in examining the topic. If the feature article lead suggests a question or poses a problem, the article should answer the question or solve the problem in the body of the writing, and the ending should point to the answer or solution.

The effective ending to a feature article comes full circle, to show that the work begun by the writer in the lead has been satisfactorily completed. The effective ending reinforces the writer's intention that is stated in the lead. Unlike the ending to the hard news article, which may introduce a future action or a fact that is not integral to the present article, the feature story ending must focus on summarizing and highlighting the article *without* repeating information or introducing new material.

Consider the different endings that might emerge in an article developed from the *description* lead example that appears in Chapter Three.

He has a black belt in karate and has trained in several other martial arts. His home is protected by an electronic surveillance system, and his children are trained never to give personal information to callers or strangers on the street. He always keeps his cars in perfect running order. Each member of his family carries a cellular phone at all times, to call for help in case of emergencies. He owns two registered handguns, one placed securely by his bedside and the other in a specially designed compartment under the driver's seat of his car.

Today, Joseph Andrews is in the intensive care ward of Metropolitan Hospital, the victim of multiple stab wounds after being attacked while he walked from his car to the office. The knife-wielding attacker surprised Mr. Andrews from behind, stabbing him in the neck and disabling him before he could defend himself.

Full-Circle Ending

The full-circle ending gives the reader a sense of completeness by pulling all elements of the article together to provide symmetry in the writing.

The experiences of many Americans who, like Joseph Andrews, have been the victims of random violence are all too common in the 1990s. Many people are frightened—for themselves and for their families—and they barricade themselves in their homes instead of confronting the problem. Rather than give in, however, society must work as a whole to make America safe again.

Climax Ending

The climax ending examines an issue throughout the article while keeping the reader in suspense to the very end.

> The fact that most victims of violence have met their attackers, even if only in passing, makes the issue even more frightening. The victim in this story had also met his attacker, many times. Joseph Andrews was stabbed by the panhandler whom he saw every morning outside his office building, and to whom he gave a dollar each day.

Cliffhanger Ending

The cliffhanger ending downplays the importance of the results of incidents discussed in the article and focuses, instead, on the issues. Thus, the fate of the subject or the resolution of an incident is not revealed.

> The world outside the hospital continues to follow its daily schedule, and the monitors in Joseph Andrews's room continue their steady hum. His chances of survival have improved since he was first brought in, but the doctors still refuse to make any promises to his wife and family.

Future Action Ending

The future action ending completes the discussion of the article and, as part of the summary statements, alludes to the next step of the issue.

> Nina Andrews and her children keep a silent vigil at the hospital, hoping that love is strong enough to keep their husband and father alive. Whether he lives or dies, they know that none of them will ever feel completely safe again.

Quote Ending

The carefully chosen quote that functions as an ending should succinctly and accurately sum up the point of the article. As in the hard news ending, the attribution should either precede or appear in the middle of the quote.

"Poor Joe," says Nina Andrews, as she holds the hand of her comatose husband and tries hard to keep back tears. "He really believed that he had every possibility covered and that we were really safe."

Factual Ending

The strong factual ending is based on fact and summarizes the mood, the tone or the intention of the article. It can easily substitute for the lead.

The attack on Joseph Andrews is not an isolated incident. Statistics show that Americans are spending more money annually for personal and home security. At the same time, violent crime is rising. No one is immune to this danger.

When all of the components of the newspaper or magazine article have been completed, you are ready to edit, revise and rewrite to create the finished article.

Chapter Ten

The Final Version

The first draft of any article is simply an unfinished product. Writers who brag that they never revise their first drafts usually have several drawers full of rejection slips and numerous stories of unpleasant dealings with editors. Do not become one of them.

Reread your article several times and make changes on the printed copy. Many experienced writers prefer to edit their writing while seated at the computer, but others prefer to edit hard copy. Either approach works for some writers, but the second is preferable if you are editing a feature article or if you are a less-experienced writer.

Newspaper articles have a short lead time, so they offer little time for repeated revisions. In contrast, the feature article often has an extended deadline, which allows the writer to run through several drafts of the work. In some cases, earlier versions of sections in a lengthy feature may work better with later versions of other sections. If you edit on hard copy and save each draft, you can then review each revision for comparison. This is not possible with on-screen editing. Once a revision is completed on a computer, earlier versions are lost unless you save the changes each time.

Try to identify the problems in your article and correct them *before* submitting it. Approach the writing as objectively as possible and assess the material based on the following questions:

1. Is the substance of the article the same as originally agreed on with the editor?
2. Does the article exhibit a consistent theme?

3. Does the article contain a consistent tone?
4. Is the voice of the article consistent?
5. Are adequate descriptive details provided to illustrate the meaning of generalizations?
6. Is the writing free of clichés and other timeworn phrases?
7. Does the writing contain strong verbs and precise words?
8. Is the organization of the content logical?
9. Are the transitions invisible, and do they allow the ideas to flow seamlessly together to form a whole?
10. Are all quotations strong and meaningful?
11. Are all quotations correctly attributed?
12. Does the lead capture your attention as a reader?
13. Does the lead connect with the rest of the article?
14. Does the ending complete the story?
15. Is the ending connected to the lead and to the rest of the story?
16. Would *you* continue to read the article after the lead?

Be brutal in assessing how well your article meets the requirements identified in the preceding questions. If you answer "No" to any questions, then make the changes necessary to eliminate the problems. Even the writer who can honestly answer "Yes" to every question cannot guarantee that the editor will agree. This list is not an exhaustive review of how to produce a publishable newspaper or magazine article. Still, the writer whose work satisfies these requirements will have to rewrite less of the article for an editor than a writer who ignores the list.

The final approach to revising your article is to read it aloud and to *listen* to the rhythm and the flow of the sentences and paragraphs. Keep in mind that the editor will hear what you hear. Therefore, correct awkward word order, rambling sentences and jarring transitions within paragraphs.

The hard-news article writer often has only a few hours in which to organize notes into a coherent article that contains the most important information first. The inverted pyramid may restrict creativity, but the form also aids writers in organizing their ideas quickly to meet the short deadlines.

In contrast, the soft news or feature article, most often published in magazines, allows writers to be more creative in organizing and developing ideas. The fewer restrictions combined with the greater length of most feature articles make care in revising even more critical. Use the time allowed by the longer deadline to edit, revise and rewrite your article until the writing becomes irresistible, even to the creator.

Glossary

Anecdotal lead   The opening paragraph(s) of an article containing a brief story that represents the theme of the work.

Angle   The specific focus or approach to the topic.

Byline   The line, usually following the title of an article, that identifies the author.

Clips   Stories physically cut from a newspaper. A writer might use clips to give evidence of writing ability.

Copy   Any writing submitted by a reporter to a newspaper or magazine.

Copy editor   The individual who reviews the submitted stories, corrects grammar and organization errors, and polishes the writing.

Cover story   Either the most important story or one of the most important stories in the magazine issue; usually listed on the cover.

Deadline   The time that assigned work is due to the editor.

Developing story   A news story that continues to generate newsworthy events over the course of several days or more.

Editorial department   The department of a newspaper that is responsible for all of the content except the advertising.

Editorialize   An undesirable action in which the writer has inserted personal opinion into a news story.

Hard lead   The opening of a news article that reports new facts or a new development.

Human-interest story   An article that is based more on emotional impact or an unusual angle than on newsworthiness.

Inverted pyramid   The widely accepted formula in hard news articles in which the most important information is placed at the beginning, followed by support in descending order of importance.

Layout   A completed page drawing, sometimes called the "dummy," provided by the editorial staff to show the composing room where the articles and pictures are to appear.

Lead   The first paragraph of a hard news article, or the first several paragraphs of a feature article, that succinctly summarizes the material that follows.

Lead story   The most important news story of the day; usually displayed at the top of page one.

News room   Also called the "city room," the place where editors and reporters work.

News value   The importance or interest level of a story.

Off the record   A statement by a speaker asking the writer to omit identifying the source of a quote.

Open-ended question   A question that requires the respondent to provide more than a mere "Yes" or "No" answer.

Open record laws   State and federal laws that provide access to most government records.

Plagiarism   A writer's use of someone else's words or ideas without giving appropriate credit.

Press   Used as a synonym for journalism; increasingly used to refer to *print* journalism.

Profile   A detailed examination of the character or essence of an individual or an institution.

Publisher   The top–ranking executive of a newspaper or magazine; the role assumed by the owner in privately held enterprises.

Quote   As a noun, the use of the exact words of a source; as a verb, to report the exact words of a source and indicate the action by placing those words within quotation marks.

Rewrite   To use already provided material, i.e., a first draft, and write it again to create a polished article.

Sidebar   An addition to the main story placed in a box on the side and containing data, facts or a more focused view of participants.

Soft lead   The opening paragraphs of a soft news or feature article that uses an anecdote, quote or other device to attract the reader's attention.

Soft news   Feature articles, usually found in magazines, that focus on human-interest concerns rather than on breaking news.

Sources People or places from which the writer obtains information.

Story The term used by both newspaper and magazine journalists to mean an article.

Summary lead The opening paragraph of an article in which the writer answers all six questions of journalists: *Who? What? When? Where? Why?* and *How?*

Transition The writer's use of a word, phrase, sentence or paragraph to move the reader from one thought to another.